LIVING *in your*
SOUL'S LIGHT

UNDERSTANDING YOUR ETERNAL SELF

RICHARD WEBSTER

About the Author

Richard Webster was born and raised in New Zealand, where he still resides with his wife and three children. He travels widely every year, lecturing and conducting workshops around the world.

Richard has been interested in the psychic world since he was nine years old and is the author of over a hundred books. His bestselling books include *Spirit Guides & Angel Guardians* and *Creative Visualization for Beginners*.

LIVING *in your*
SOUL'S LIGHT

UNDERSTANDING YOUR ETERNAL SELF

RICHARD WEBSTER

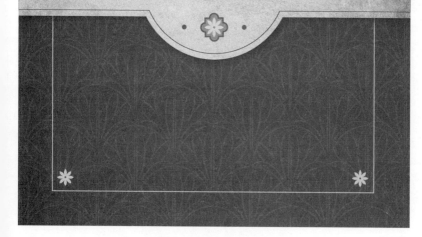

Llewellyn Publications
Woodbury, Minnesota

FIRST EDITION
First Printing, 2012

Book design by Donna Burch
Cover art ©: Background pattern: iStockphoto.com/Olga Dmitrishena
           Mandala: iStockphoto.com/Heidi Kalyani
Cover design by Kevin R. Brown
Editing by Andrea Neff
Interior illustrations by the Llewellyn Art Department

Llewellyn Publications is a registered trademark of Llewellyn Worldwide Ltd.

Library of Congress Cataloging-in-Publication Data
Webster, Richard, 1946–
  Living in your soul's light : understanding your eternal self / by Richard Webster.
  — 1st ed.
     p. cm.
  Includes bibliographical references and index.
  ISBN 978-0-7387-3249-7
1. Reincarnation. 2. Soul. 3. Future life. I. Title.
  BL515.W384 2012
  133.901'35—dc23
                       2012010693

Llewellyn Publications
A Division of Llewellyn Worldwide Ltd.
2143 Wooddale Drive
Woodbury, MN 55125-2989
www.llewellyn.com

Printed in the United States of America

Other Books by Richard Webster

Astral Travel for Beginners

Aura Reading for Beginners

Candle Magic for Beginners

Color Magic for Beginners

Creative Visualization for Beginners

Dowsing for Beginners

The Encyclopedia of Superstitions

Feng Shui for Beginners

Flower and Tree Magic

Gabriel

Geomancy for Beginners

Is Your Pet Psychic?

Magical Symbols of Love & Romance

Michael

Miracles

Palm Reading for Beginners

Pendulum Magic for Beginners

Practical Guide to Past-Life Memories

Praying with Angels

Psychic Protection for Beginners

Raphael

Soul Mates

Spirit & Dream Animals

Spirit Guides & Angel Guardians

Uriel

Write Your Own Magic

Dedication

For my good friends
Paul and Natalie Romhany

Contents

INTRODUCTION

A COUPLE OF YEARS ago I was rushed to the hospital late one evening. I had felt well all day, and my wife and I had enjoyed a barbecue dinner that evening. However, after dinner I noticed a slight discomfort on my left side. This gradually got worse, and after a few hours I started having problems with my breathing, so my wife called an ambulance. I was misdiagnosed twice before the doctors discovered I had two large blood clots in my lungs.

I remember nothing of the following two days. On the third evening I woke up in the middle of the night with tubes attached to both arms and a small box on my chest that transmitted information about me to a computer somewhere else in the building. Five doctors and nurses surrounded the bed. I stared at the five pairs of eyes gazing down on me and thought, *I must be sick*. I immediately fell back to sleep.

When I woke up the following morning, I was disappointed that I hadn't seen any tunnels leading to the light or any other signs of a near-death experience. All the same, I was grateful to be alive. I also woke up with the title of this book in my mind, and the thought refused to go away. I spent another week in the hospital before being allowed to return home. It was a frustrating time, as all I wanted to do was leave the hospital and start writing.

Of course, it wasn't as simple as that. It took time to get my energy back, and then I had to finish the project I'd been working on before going to the hospital. Consequently, more than three months passed before I was able to start work on this book.

I also had time in the hospital to think about life and death. I was extremely fortunate. Apparently, sixty percent of the people who suffer from a pulmonary embolism are dead within twenty-four hours, and a large number of the survivors suffer from strokes and heart attacks.

I have no fear of death, as I don't believe death is the end. It simply marks the end of one stage of existence and the start of the next. I came to this conclusion for five main reasons:

1. For many years I worked as a hypnotherapist and helped many people recover memories of their past lives. Some people's lives were rather vague, but others provided detailed accounts of their previous incarna-

tions. In a few cases the people were able to revisit the places where they had lived before, and instantly felt at home.

2. The research of Dr. Ian Stevenson, and many other researchers, into children who remember their past lives has produced convincing evidence of reincarnation. I have a small personal example of this, too. For as long as I can remember, I've had a memory of being a small child, with a full stomach, lying in front of a huge fire with large red circles revolving around it. Years before becoming interested in reincarnation, I accidentally knocked a volume from a set of encyclopedias onto the floor. The book opened at a photograph of Russian peasant women dancing around an open fire. Although their skirts were black, the interior lining was red, and it must have been this that I remembered.

3. Although I haven't had a near-death experience myself, I've read many books about people's near-death experiences and am fascinated with what they saw, felt, and experienced on the "other side." I also find it convincing that very similar near-death experiences have been recorded from all around the world.

4. There is ample evidence of life after death provided by mediums who have communicated with people on the other side. This may sound surprising, but for at least 2,500 years thousands of messages have been recorded, all around the world, by people who claim

they have received messages from the other side.[1] One of the most evidential of these was William Stainton Moses (1839–1892), an English clergyman who was unhappy with the un-Christian teachings that came through him in the form of automatic writing. Automatic writing occurs when the person's mind is at ease, and the writing does not come from his or her conscious mind. William Stainton Moses wrote four books, including *Spirit Teachings*.[2]

5. Most major religions teach that life continues after death. Christians, for instance, teach that believers in God will go to heaven, but agnostics, atheists, and members of other religions will not. In Islam, the righteous will experience all the joys and pleasures of paradise, but everyone else will go to hell. Hindus also have a heaven and a hell. Reincarnation is an integral part of Buddhist belief, and everyone has to experience many lifetimes before they can return home. Judaism is the only major religion that is vague about what happens after death. However, it teaches that good people will be rewarded and evil people punished.

Obviously, we leave our body behind when we die. However, our soul carries on.

The soul is the immortal or divine aspect of our being. It is present in every cell of our body and continues to exist after the physical body dies. The soul could be described as the software that enables a computer to function. In this instance, the computer would be the physical body that is lifeless unless it contains a soul (software). Many religious people believe the soul is the presence of God inside each and every one of us.

People have been preoccupied with death, and the possibility of life after death, for thousands of years. Most early civilizations believed in life after death, and that belief is just as popular today as it ever was. When someone died, the ancient Neanderthals buried food and weapons with the body, as they believed the person's soul would need those items in the next world.

The ancient Greeks believed that to be fully alive, you needed a soul. The Greek word *psyche* means both "alive" and "possessing a soul."

The soul played an important role in Orphism, a Greek religion said to have been founded by the legendary musician, poet, and prophet Orpheus. Practitioners believed the physical body was dirty and corrupt, but the soul was perfect and part of the Divine. The soul became truly alive only after the death of the body. To achieve total freedom, the soul had to reincarnate many times. Depending on the quality of the person's life, the soul would be reborn in either a higher or lower form of life.

Pythagoras (c. 570–c. 490 BCE) was a Greek philosopher, numerologist, and teacher who believed that the cosmos followed certain moral and numerological principles. He was best known for his teachings on the soul. According to Pythagoras, who claimed to remember his own past lives, the soul was immortal and underwent a series of reincarnations.

Xenophanes (c. 570–c. 480 BCE), the Greek poet and philosopher, wrote of an occasion when Pythagoras heard the yelping of a puppy who was being punished. He ordered the beating to cease, as he realized the dog possessed the soul of a deceased friend. This shows that Pythagoras believed human souls could be reincarnated into plants, animals, or humans, a belief called *metempsychosis*. Not surprisingly, Pythagoras was a vegetarian.

Herodotus (c. 485–425 BCE), the Greek historian, wrote that the ancient Egyptians believed the soul was reborn time and time again until it had lived a lifetime as every possible animal before returning to human form three thousand years later. However, there is no evidence, apart from his writings, to confirm this. Herodotus also wrote that the bodies of dead Athenians who were killed at the siege of Potidaea were committed to the ground, but their souls flew upward.[3]

Plato (c. 428–347 BCE) recorded and developed the teachings of his mentor, Socrates (469–399 BCE). Plato believed the soul was the person's spiritual essence. It survived the person's death and was reincarnated inside another body. Plato and Socrates both thought that no harm could come to someone who kept his or her integrity, as this person's soul remained unharmed. Someone who deliberately hurt others damaged his or her soul. Consequently, it was better to be a victim of injustice than to commit an act of injustice.

In his dialogue *Phaedo*, Plato wrote that both the *psyche* (the life force) and the *nous* (the mind) were immortal. Together, the psyche and the nous formed the soul. In *Phaedrus*, another of his dialogues, the soul, released from the dead body, raced heavenward but failed to reach the home of the gods. It fell back to Earth and was reincarnated. The soul continued to do this until it was finally reunited with the Divine. This reveals Plato's belief that everything possesses a strong desire to return home to the ultimate life force. Even the earth itself (the "world-soul") longs to return home.

Aristotle (384–322 BCE) considered the soul to be the essential essence or nature of a person, but did not accept that it could continue to exist separate from the physical body. He believed the soul provided the person's personality and intellect while he or she was alive, but did not carry on after the person had died. In his treatise *De Anima (On the Soul)*, Aristotle argued that although the soul was the essential essence of a living organism and was necessary for life to exist, it did not possess a shape and consequently could not be measured or seen. Aristotle believed the soul took on the form of the body. However, by this he meant that the soul existed in every cell of the body.

Posidonius (c. 135–c. 51 BCE) was a Greek philosopher, historian, and Stoic. Most Stoics believed that the soul died with the body, but Posidonius had a different point of view. He believed that the soul continued to live in the air until the next major world calamity occurred. There was no hell in his system, but evil people did not fare as well as good people. Any sin affected the soul and discolored it, making it impossible for a sinful soul to rise as high as a pure soul. The souls of extremely evil people remained close to Earth and were reincarnated. Conversely, the souls of extremely virtuous people rose so high that they could watch the movements of the stars. From this position, they could help other souls.[4]

Plotinus (c. 205–270), the Greek philosopher and founder of Neoplatonism, developed a concept of "One" that he considered the essential underlying structure of all existence. As "One" was spiritual and nonmaterial, it could not be understood or fully explained. Plotinus claimed that "One" was both all things and nothing. Consequently, it could live both within and outside the world at the same time. "One" also provided humans with minds, intellects, and souls. The soul was, in effect, trapped inside the body, as it constantly sought union with the "One." Although this was the soul's true destiny, many people focused on their sensual desires, which caused the soul to descend, or move further away from the "One." When this occurred, the soul did not return to the "One," and entered another body. Plotinus had a strong influence on early Christian theology.

Avicenna (c. 980–1037), the Persian philosopher and physician, is best known today for his *Canon of Medicine*, which is arguably the most famous book in the history of medicine. However, in addition to this, he wrote more than two hundred works on a variety of topics, including philosophy and religion. He was deeply interested in Aristotle's ideas, and introduced many of them to the Islamic world. He agreed with Aristotle that the soul originated from the heart. He believed that, although the soul was immortal, this was purely an aspect of its nature rather than its prime purpose.

Avicenna lived in difficult times and was imprisoned on at least two occasions. While in prison, Avicenna wrote about an experiment his readers could try for themselves. This has become known as the "flying man" experiment. Avicenna told his readers to imagine they were suspended in space, temporarily blind and totally isolated from any sensation, including their own bodies. In this instance, Avicenna wrote that the person would not be able to affirm the existence of his or her own body but would still possess consciousness. This, he concluded, demonstrated that the soul was an essential part of humankind's nature, and everyone possessed it from birth.

St. Thomas Aquinas (1225–1274), the Italian philosopher and theologian, was a prolific author who tried to harmonize Aristotle's philosophical rationalism with Christianity. He claimed that the soul was the first principle of life and that people possessed both a body and a soul. He argued that, because the soul was not composed of matter, it could continue to exist outside a human body.[5] St. Thomas Aquinas agreed with Aristotle that the soul was present in every part of the body.

Immanuel Kant (1724–1804), the German philosopher, believed that perfect good could exist only if the soul was immortal. He believed in *unendlichen progressus*, the unending progression of the soul through countless incarnations.

Sir Edward Tylor (1832–1917) was the first professor of anthropology at Oxford University. In his two-volume work *Primitive Culture*, he demonstrated that human culture constantly grows and develops, following specific laws of evolutionary development. He developed a theory of animism, which he described as "the doctrine of souls and other spiritual beings in general." Animism is derived from the Latin word *anima*, which means "breath" or "soul." Tylor described the soul as:

> ... a thin insubstantial image, in its nature a sort of vapour, film or shadow; the cause of life and thought in the individual it animates; independently possessing the personal consciousness and volition of its corporeal owner, past or present; capable of leaving the body far behind, to flash swiftly from place to place; mostly impalpable and invisible, yet also manifesting physical power, and especially appearing to man walking or asleep as a phantasm separate from the body of which it bears the likeness; continuing to exist and appear to man after the death of that body; able to enter into, possess, and act in the bodies of other men, of animals, and even of things.[6]

Carl Jung (1875–1961), the Swiss psychiatrist and psychologist, described the soul as "the greatest of all cosmic miracles."[7]

Belief in the soul is probably more common in the East than in the West, and the concepts of reincarnation and karma are accepted more readily there than in the West. Reincarnation requires a soul, as it is the belief that the soul is eternal and is reborn into a new personality once the current life has ended. The soul learns from every incarnation as it progresses on its journey to oneness with God.

In chapter 1 we'll look into the concept of reincarnation and learn three methods you can use to examine your past lives.

CHAPTER ONE

HAVE I MET YOU BEFORE?

REINCARNATION IS THE BELIEF that after death some part of the self, usually the soul, is reborn in a new body.

My interest in the soul began many years ago, when I was working as a hypnotherapist. Many of my clients requested a past-life regression to help them remember information about their previous lives. I was fascinated with the amount of detail some people were able to recall. A few of my clients traveled overseas to visit the places where they had lived in a previous lifetime. Some of them returned with information that confirmed, at least in their minds, that they had lived in that place at some time in the past.

Some people came for a past-life regression out of curiosity. Without exception, all of them found the experience

helpful in explaining factors in their current life. Someone who was terrified of water, for instance, learned that
she'd drowned in a previous lifetime. A man who loved the
works of Franz Joseph Haydn learned that he'd worked in
the court of Prince Miklós Esterházy at the same time as
the great composer, and was introduced to his music there.
Someone who was abused by his father when he was a child
discovered that he had been the abuser in a previous lifetime.

Many people ask for a past-life regression to see if certain people in this lifetime figured in previous incarnations.
Often this is the case, even though the nature of the relationship, and even the gender of the people involved, sometimes change.

Many of my clients discovered that the person they love
the most in this lifetime is a true soul mate, as they have
been together in a number of previous lifetimes. Interestingly, they may not have been together in every incarnation. Usually some impediment prevented them from being
together in a particular lifetime. One person may have
already been married, for instance. I recall one sad example
where the man was a priest and unable to enter into a relationship.

It seems that people who share a deep spiritual and emotional bond are always together, both while in a relationship
on earth and in the period between lives. These people also
incarnate at approximately the same time and are exposed to
opportunities where they can meet and carry on their rela-

tionship. One couple I regressed had almost met on several occasions, in three different countries, before finally meeting (or re-meeting) each other. It seems the universe works to enable soul mates to meet and continue their relationship in each incarnation.

I have met a number of people who dislike the idea of reincarnation. "I don't want to be reborn," they tell me. "Once is enough!"

Fortunately, people do not reincarnate as the people they are today. Their physical body, mind, and emotions die. It is their soul that carries on and reincarnates into a new body and personality.

Another common question is "Why can't I remember my past lives?" I think it's fortunate that we can't. If we remembered details from all our previous lifetimes, we'd never be able to progress in this incarnation. Some people spontaneously remember incidents from their past lives, and many instances of these have been recorded.[1] Many people have a vague sense that they have lived before. The poem "Sudden Light" by Dante Gabriel Rossetti (1828–1882) captures these feelings extremely well:

> I have been here before,
> But when or how I cannot tell:
> I know the grass beyond the door,
> The sweet keen smell,
> The sighing sound, the lights around the shore.
>
> You have been mine before,—
> How long ago I may not know:

But just when at the swallow's soar
Your neck turned so,
Some veil did fall,—I knew it all of yore.

Another logical question is "Why do we reincarnate?" Even people who lead outwardly happy lives sometimes feel there must be more to life than constantly striving for worldly success. What's the point of living for five, six, or seven decades if you, and everything you've accomplished, are forgotten in a few generations?

Reincarnation enables us to experience a wide range of possibilities as we progress from one lifetime to the next and become increasingly aware of our divine nature. It is impossible to do this in just one lifetime, as we all face various limitations, including gender, family circumstances, race, color, intelligence, natural skills, and personality. Hopefully we progress spiritually in each incarnation until we eventually return to our "source," which is God.

William Wordsworth refers to "God, who is our home" in his ode "Intimations of Immortality":

Our birth is but a sleep and a forgetting:
The Soul that rises with us, our life's Star,
Hath had elsewhere its setting,
And cometh from afar:
Not in entire forgetfulness,
And not in utter nakedness,
But trailing clouds of glory do we come
From God, who is our home.

There have been many recorded instances of people remembering their previous incarnations. Dr. Ian Stevenson (1918–2007), former head of the Division of Perceptual Studies at the University of Virginia, investigated more than three thousand cases of children who appeared to remember their past lives. He traveled extensively to research these cases and wrote several books about his findings.

One of the many examples Dr. Stevenson collected was told to him by Ravi Shankar, an Indian boy who vividly recalled his previous life as Munna Prasad. On January 19, 1951, Munna Prasad was lured away from his friends by two neighbors who killed him with a knife or razor. His head and body were buried separately. Munna was only six years old.

One of the alleged murderers, a barber named Jawahar, apparently killed Munna because he was the only son of Sri Jageshwar Prasad. This meant that Jawahar would inherit property that would otherwise have been left to Munna. Neighbors had seen Munna being taken away by the two men, and they were arrested. One of them, a washerman named Chaturi, confessed to the murder but then retracted his confession after being officially charged. As there were no witnesses to the murder, the case was dropped and the two men were released from custody.

A few years later, the dead boy's father heard about a boy who had been born six months after Munna's death. This boy, Ravi Shankar, said he was the son of Jageshwar and could clearly remember his life and death as Munna. He was even able to name the murderers and describe the place where he had been killed.

Ravi Shankar's mother and his older sister remembered that when he was two years old he repeatedly asked for toys that he remembered having in his previous life. When he was five years old, he described his murder in great detail to his schoolteacher, who recorded the conversation in a letter. He told the teacher he had eaten some guavas before meeting his friends, when he was enticed away by two men who killed him in an orchard near the river by the Chintamani Temple and then buried him in the sand. He knew his throat had been cut with a razor.

Naturally, Sri Jageshwar Prasad, Munna's father, wanted to learn more. He visited the home of Ravi Shankar, but Ravi's father, fearing that Jageshwar might take his son, refused to talk with him. Fortunately, Ravi's mother allowed Jageshwar to talk with Ravi, who provided a full account of the murder. He recognized Munna's watch and asked what had happened to his ring. He also recognized Munna's maternal grandmother, who was with a group of other women.

Ravi was born with a strange birthmark on his neck. When Dr. Stevenson saw it in 1964, he described it as looking "much like an old scar of a healed knife wound."[2]

Ravi's father was concerned about his son's constant fixation on his previous lifetime, and beat him severely whenever he talked about it. After this, Ravi became afraid to talk about his experiences. However, he was overcome with fear when he happened to see one of the men who had allegedly killed Munna. He was also afraid of barbers and washermen. When Ravi continued to discuss certain aspects of his murder with his neighbors, his father sent him away for a year.

By the time he was eleven, Ravi had forgotten most of the events of his previous life. However, he still became frightened whenever he saw Chaturi or Jawahar, the two men who allegedly murdered Munna.[3]

It is common for children who remember their previous lives to gradually forget them as they grow up. It is less common for spontaneous past-life memories to unexpectedly return.

This happened to General George S. Patton (1885–1945), the famous American hero of World War II. When he arrived at the French town of Langres, his driver offered to show him around the well-preserved Roman ruins. "You don't have to," the general replied. "I know this place. I know it well."[4]

He then took the driver on a tour of the Roman remains, indicating the drill ground, the forum, the amphitheatre, and the temples of Mars and Apollo. Visiting Langres brought back memories of General Patton's past life as a legionary in Caesar's army.

Not surprisingly, General Patton believed in reincarnation, and remembered several previous lifetimes. He remembered fighting with Alexander the Great. He spent a lifetime as the great Carthaginian general Hannibal. He also recalled being part of a Greek contingent that met the Persian conqueror Cyrus II around 500 BCE. He remembered fighting in the Hundred Years' War, and served as a general with Joachim Murat, one of Napoleon's most honored marshals.

One year before he died, General Patton wrote a poem called "Through a Glass, Darkly," which clearly illustrated his Christian faith as well as his belief in reincarnation. Here is one verse from the poem:

> *So as through a glass, and darkly*
> *The age-long strife I see*
> *Where I fought in many guises,*
> *Many names, but always me.*[5]

Most reincarnation memories are faint and fragmentary. However, a few accounts are incredibly detailed and convincing. The story of Corliss Chotkin Jr. is a good example.

Victor Vincent was a full-blooded Tlingit Indian who lived in Angoon, Alaska. He had a close relationship with his niece, Mrs. Corliss Chotkin. One year before he died in 1946, Victor told his niece that he would return as her next son. She would recognize him, he said, because the baby would have two scars on his body that matched surgical scars he had received. Eighteen months after Victor died, his niece gave birth to a son who was named after his father, Corliss Chotkin. The baby had two birthmarks that were identical to the two scars Victor had had.

When Corliss was thirteen months old and starting to talk, his family tried to teach him his name. Corliss suddenly spoke in a Tlingit accent: "Don't you know me? I'm Kahkody." This was Victor Vincent's tribal name.

When Corliss was two, he was out with his mother when they came across a woman he hadn't met before. He immediately became excited, saying, "There's my Susie." Susie was Victor Vincent's stepdaughter. Corliss hugged her, called her by her Tlingit name, and kept saying, "My Susie, my Susie!"

A few weeks later, Corliss and his mother were out for a walk, and Corliss said, "There is William, my son." Mrs. Chotkin hadn't noticed William Vincent, Victor's son, until Corliss pointed to him.

A year later, when Corliss was three, he and his mother went to a meeting, and Corliss called out, "There's Rose" and "That's the old lady." Rose was Victor Vincent's widow, and he'd always called her "the old lady." Corliss's mother had not known Rose was at the meeting until Corliss said her name.

In addition to recognizing family members, Corliss frequently recognized Victor Vincent's friends, and spoke of various incidents that had occurred in his previous life. On one occasion, he and his mother visited a house that Mrs. Chotkin had lived in while Victor Vincent was alive. Corliss pointed out the room that he and "the old lady" had slept in when they had stayed overnight.

One day Corliss told his parents about an incident that had happened in his previous life. He (Victor) was out fishing when his engine broke down. This was potentially life-threatening in the cold waters of southeast Alaska. Victor was a part-time worker for the Salvation Army. He changed into his uniform to help attract attention and got into a small rowboat. His unusual clothing, plus the fact that he was in a small dinghy, caused a passing ship, the North Star, to rescue him. Corliss's mother had heard Victor tell this story and was amazed to hear it again, in complete detail, from her young son.

By the time Corliss was nine, memories of his previous life started to fade. When Dr. Ian Stevenson met him in 1962, the fifteen-year-old told him he remembered nothing of his previous life.[6]

Edgar Cayce (1877–1945) was the most famous American psychic of the twentieth century. At the age of sixteen, he injured his spine. While in a coma, he suddenly spoke in a strong, clear voice, prescribing himself an herbal remedy. The attending doctor agreed to give this alternative medicine a try, and when Cayce woke up the following morning, he was fit and well again.

When he was twenty-four, Cayce lost his voice, and doctors were unable to do anything to help. Cayce was desperate and asked a friend to put him into a hypnotic trance. In this state Cayce prescribed himself a cure, which worked just as well as the herbal remedy he'd prescribed himself before. Gradually word spread about this unusual ability, and before long local physicians started asking him for help in diagnosing and treating difficult cases. His fame increased dramatically when the *New York Times* wrote an article about him in October 1910.

Cayce's workload increased so much that he was forced to hire a stenographer, who wrote down everything he said while in a trance state. On August 10, 1923, Cayce, a fundamentalist Christian, was alarmed to read that he had proclaimed the reality of reincarnation while in trance. At that time he had no interest in the subject, and considered it anti-Christian.

Two months later, on October 11, 1923, Cayce mentioned a client's previous incarnation. "Third appearance on this plane," he said while in trance. "He was once a monk."[7]

Cayce gradually reconciled reincarnation with his Christian faith, and his readings frequently traced people's problems back to previous lifetimes. In fact, he talked about people's previous lives in more than 1,900 of his life readings. Cayce even uncovered two of his own past incarnations. In about 10,500 BCE, he had been a Carpathian priest named Ra-Ta at the time his tribe conquered Egypt. In 1742, he was born again as John Bainbridge in Cornwall, England. He led a highly adventurous life in America, and died on a raft floating down the Ohio River while helping a group of people escape from an Indian attack.[8]

Although there is no way to prove reincarnation, the numerous accounts of people remembering their past lives have created a huge body of anecdotal evidence that cannot be ignored.

Many famous people throughout history have believed in reincarnation. Benjamin Franklin is a good example. When he was just twenty-two, Franklin wrote his epitaph:

The body of B. Franklin,
Printer,
Like the Cover of an old Book,
Its Contents Torn Out
And
Stripped of its Lettering and Gilding,
Lies Here
Food for Worms,
But the Work shall not be Lost,
For it Will as He Believed
Appear Once More
In a New and more Elegant Edition
Revised and Corrected
By the Author.

Charles C. Emerson (1808–1836), Ralph Waldo Emerson's younger brother, was, like his brother, a strong believer in reincarnation. He wrote:

The reason why Homer is to me like a dewy morning is because I too lived while Troy was, and sailed in the hollow ships of the Grecians to sack the devoted town. The rosy-fingered dawn as it crimsoned the tops of Ida, the broad seashore covered with tents, the Trojan hosts in their painted armor, and the rushing chariots of Diomede and Idomeneus,—all these I too saw: my ghost animated the frame of some nameless Argive … We forget that we have been drugged by the sleepy bowl of the present.

But when a lively chord in the soul is struck, when the windows for a moment are unbarred, the long and varied past is recovered. We recognize it all; we are not mere brief ignoble creatures; we seize our immortality and bind together the related parts of our secular beings ... Something there is in the spirit which changes not, neither is weary, but ever returns into itself, and partakes the eternity of God.[9]

How to Experience Your Past Lives

You can explore your own past lives. Some people find this difficult to do, but in my experience, everyone can learn to do it. Once you've returned to a past lifetime, you'll have no difficulty repeating it whenever you wish. The method I prefer is hypnosis. If you've had no previous experience with hypnosis, you might want to find a competent hypnotherapist in your area who performs past-life regressions. You may have to phone a few people, as not all hypnotherapists are interested in doing these. Once you've been hypnotized by a certified hypnotherapist and relived a few incidents from a previous lifetime, you'll have no difficulty hypnotizing yourself and learning more about that lifetime, or possibly looking at other previous lives.

If you're unable to find a competent hypnotherapist or prefer to experiment on your own, you'll need to hypnotize yourself. This is called self-hypnosis, and is a useful skill to learn.

Hypnosis is not something to be afraid of. Like everyone else, you go into and out of hypnosis many times every day. Every time you have a daydream, for instance, you are in a state of hypnosis. I'm sure you know people who get hypnotized whenever they watch television. You can speak to them and they don't hear a word you're saying, because they're in a state of hypnosis. Many people cry at sad movies. In every case, they were hypnotized. The fact that they cried shows they were emotionally involved in the movie, even though they knew it was simply a picture on a screen. I can get lost in a book. This means I've been hypnotized by the words I'm reading.

Possibly the most common form of unconscious hypnosis occurs when you're driving your car along a route that you know extremely well. When you arrive at your destination, you may wonder how you got there, as you have no conscious memory of the trip you've just completed. This is known as "wild" hypnosis. Fortunately, although you're in a state of hypnosis, you'd instantly come out of it if anything happened that needed your attention.

Hypnosis is similar to meditation. You are physically relaxed in both meditation and hypnosis. However, in hypnosis your mind is focused on a particular goal, such as retrieving memories of a previous lifetime. Here is a past-life regression script you can experiment with. You can use it in three different ways.

1. You can record the script and play it back when you are ready to experience a past life.

2. You can familiarize yourself with the script and then use your own words to silently guide you through the past life.

3. You can ask a friend to read the script out loud while you relive a past life. Afterwards, you can change roles.

There are advantages and disadvantages with each of these options. A recording may rush you through different scenes more rapidly than you would like. However, a recording is convenient, as all you need to do is relax and follow the instructions.

The second scenario has advantages, too, but it's easy for random thoughts to get in the way. It's also easy to forget what you're supposed to think next.

The third scenario is ideal, as long as you have a good friend who is also interested in exploring his or her past lives. Your friend won't rush you through the session and will let you stay at certain places for as long as you're continuing to tell him or her about them. However, you'll need to say your responses out loud, to let your friend know when to move forward.

With all three scenarios, you'll need to make yourself as comfortable as possible. I like to do this while relaxing in a recliner chair, as I tend to fall asleep when lying on a bed. I'm also happy to do this while lying on the floor. I can relax there, but I don't fall asleep. Cover yourself with a blanket, as you lose one or two degrees of body heat when you're in a state of hypnosis.

You should also wear loose-fitting clothes and ensure the room is warm enough. Once you're comfortable, close your eyes and start listening to the script.

Past-Life Regression Script

"Take a nice, deep breath, and exhale slowly. Allow all the muscles of your body to relax. Each breath makes you more and more relaxed, taking you deeper and deeper into pleasant relaxation. Allow the relaxation to spread through your body each time you inhale, and allow the tension and stress to dissolve and disappear each time you exhale.

"Relax more and more as you listen to the sound of my voice. Nothing need bother or disturb you, as you go deeper and deeper into pleasant relaxation.

"Soon you'll notice your feet are becoming relaxed. They'll feel loose and limp and so, so relaxed. Allow that pleasant feeling of relaxation to drift up into your legs now, and become aware of how relaxed they are. Relax your arms and hands, and feel all the stress and strain of the day slipping away from you. Soon you'll experience the wonderful sensation of complete and total relaxation throughout your entire body.

"Allow the pleasant feeling of total peace and tranquility to start in your feet and drift up through your entire body. Feel it moving up through your legs and thighs, and notice they're relaxing even more than before. Feel it drifting up into your abdomen and carrying on into your chest, your shoulders, your arms, and your neck. Allow it to drift into your head and face. Notice how relaxed the fine muscles around your eyes are becoming. Feel the relaxation drift right up to the top of your head. You feel totally loose, limp, and relaxed.

"In this nice, calm, relaxed state, become aware of your breathing. Each breath helps you drift even deeper into pleasant relaxation. It's a wonderful, soothing, peaceful sensation, and you enjoy noticing this incredible feeling of complete and total relaxation spreading all through you.

"As you let go more and more, you find yourself drifting even deeper into a peaceful state where nothing can disturb or bother you. You want to feel this pleasant relaxation in every cell of your body, and you can do this by letting go completely, letting go, and allowing the relaxation to spread through you again, all the way from the tips of your toes to the top of your head.

"Enjoy the sensation of complete and total relaxation for a moment. It's so peaceful and pleasant that you want to go even deeper, and you find you can go even deeper than you are now. Your whole body is becoming loose, limp, and so, so relaxed. Allow the relaxation in your feet to drift up into your legs, your thighs, your abdomen, your chest, and your neck. Allow it to drift down your arms to the very tips of your fingers. And allow this wonderful relaxation to drift into your head and face.

"It's a wonderful feeling to be so relaxed, and in this nice, calm, peaceful, relaxed state, your only desire is to recapture memories of one of your many past lives. In your inner mind, your subconscious mind, are all the memories of your previous lives, and in this nice, calm, peaceful, relaxed state you'll be able to unlock those memories and relive them.

"In your imagination now, visualize a beautiful staircase that leads down to what appears to be a large ballroom. Place your hand on the handrail, and allow yourself to double your relaxation with each step you take as you go down this beautiful staircase.

"Ten. Moving down one step and doubling your relaxation.

"Nine. Every breath you take is making you more and more relaxed. Drifting even deeper as you take another step.

"Eight. You are so relaxed now as you take another step down into a world of total and complete relaxation.

"Seven. Taking another step and feeling so peaceful, and calm, and relaxed.

"Six. Going even deeper now, and floating down as you quietly listen. Floating gently down one more step.

"Five. You're halfway down this beautiful staircase and feeling so, so relaxed as you take another step.

"Four. You're almost there now. Drifting down deeper and deeper with each easy breath you take.

"Three. S-o-o-o-o r-e-l-a-x-e-d. Taking another step down and doubling your relaxation once again.

"Two. Almost there. Almost at the bottom of this beautiful staircase.

"One. Taking one more step and moving into the beautiful room. Feeling good and so totally relaxed.

"And now it's time for you to explore this beautiful room. It's the most beautiful room you've ever been in, and you marvel at the beautiful carpet, the luxurious furnishings, the artwork, and the soft, gentle lighting. You even look up and admire the gorgeous ceiling. It really is an unbelievably beautiful room.

"As you walk around the room, notice all the closed doors. All the doors are different, yet they harmonize perfectly with the décor of your special room. You realize that each door lets you experience one of your many past lives. Allow yourself to take as long as you wish to decide which door you want to open. If you have a particular past life that you wish to explore, allow yourself to be guided to the correct door. If you've visited here before and want to explore a particular lifetime in greater depth, you'll instinctively know which door to open. If you haven't visited this room before and have no specific lifetime to examine, simply allow yourself to choose a door that appeals to you. When you open it, memories of the past life that has the most relevance to you in your present incarnation will come into your mind.

"There's no hurry. Take all the time you need to choose a door. [Pause for ten seconds.] Now you're looking at the door you've chosen. Take three slow, deep breaths. One. That's right. Nice, even, deep breaths. Two. Gaining confidence and strength. Three. Relaxing totally.

"You're now ready to open the door and experience some important incidents from one of your past lives. You'll remain calm and detached. Your emotions will not be affected, no matter what you experience. You can move away from any scenes you find disturbing, and if in your imagination you request a happy scene, you'll instantly find yourself there. You can return to your present life any time you wish by simply counting from one to five and opening your eyes.

"And now it's time to open the door. You'll walk in and find yourself in a situation that tells you how you spend most of your time. Walk in and familiarize yourself with the situation you find yourself in.

"Look down at your feet and see what you're wearing. Look at your clothes and your hands. Gradually become accustomed to where you are and what you're doing. [Pause for sixty seconds.]

[If someone is reading the script to you, he or she can start asking questions at this stage. Typical questions are: "Are you indoors or outside?" "Are other people here with you?" "Are you male or female?" "What is your name?" "What are you doing?" "Are you happy?"]

"Now it's time to move into a situation with the person who is most important to you in this lifetime we're exploring. On the count of three, vivid memories will return. One … two … three. [Pause for sixty seconds.]

[If someone is reading the script to you, he or she can ask questions at this stage, such as: "Describe the person." "What relationship do the two of you have?" "Why is this person so special?" "What is his/her name?"]

"And now we'll move on to a family scene. On the count of three, vivid memories will return relating to your home and family life. One … two … three. [Pause for sixty seconds.]

"Now it's time to relive a scene in which you were honored or felt proud. On the count of three. One … two … three. [Pause for sixty seconds.]

"And now it's time to find out where you lived and in what time period. If you don't know, simply allow letters and numbers to come into your mind. One … two … three. [Pause for sixty seconds.]

"On the count of three, you'll find yourself on the very last day of the lifetime you're now exploring. You will not have passed over into spirit, and you'll see yourself in a totally detached way. You won't experience any emotion or pain. One … two … three. [Pause for sixty seconds.]

[If someone is reading the script, he or she can ask questions, such as: "What are you wearing?" "Who is there with you?" "How old are you?"]

"On the count of three again, it will be just a few moments after you've passed over into spirit in this lifetime we're exploring. One … two … three. [Pause for sixty seconds.]

"And now I'd like you to think about the lifetime you've been exploring and see what karma, or anything else, from that lifetime is affecting your current life. On the count of three, all sorts of thoughts will come into your conscious mind. One … two … three. [Pause for sixty seconds.]

"Now it's time to leave this past life and return to your current life. I'm going to count from one to five, and you'll be back in the present, relaxing quietly with your eyes closed. You'll return to your current life, remembering everything that happened during this lifetime, and more memories will come into your conscious mind over the next few days. It's time to return to the present on the count of five. One ... two ... three ... four ... five.

"You're now back in your current life and I'm going to count from one to five again. When I reach number five, you'll open your eyes feeling relaxed and refreshed, as if you've just enjoyed a really good night's sleep. However, this session will not affect your sleep tonight. You'll sleep extremely well. Gradually coming up now on the count of five. One. Gaining energy, and feeling fine. Two. Feeling good. Very, very good. Three. Recalling who you are, and where you are. Four. Almost there. And five. Eyes opening, and feeling wonderful."

Lie quietly for a minute or two before stretching and getting up. If possible, have something to eat or drink within ten minutes of completing the regression.

Everyone responds to a past-life regression in their own way. Some people feel slightly sad, especially if the past life was an unhappy one. Some people are excited, as the experience has explained certain things that have happened in their current life. Some people recognize important people in their current life as figures in their previous life. The relationships, and even genders, might have changed, but these people were clearly recognizable. These people are soul mates who appear in many, if not all, of the person's past lives.

As you can see, listening to a recording is not always the best way to experience a past life. Sixty seconds may be too long, or too short, to spend examining a certain scene. However, there is no reason you can't record a different tape and revisit the same past life with different questions.

When I used to do one-on-one past-life regressions, I would sometimes take people to their funeral, or to visit their burial site, so they could read what was on the headstone. This clarified dates of birth and death. Hundreds of years ago, most people were illiterate and never traveled far from home. Consequently, they often did not know the name of the country they lived in or the time period. Seeing their headstone sometimes answered these questions.

Once you've experienced a past-life regression, you'll find you'll be able to repeat it whenever you wish.

There's no danger in doing this. I find it fascinating that you can be in the middle of a past-life regression and still be aware of sounds and smells from your present life. The phone may ring, a noisy car may pass your home, and you may smell dinner cooking in the kitchen. Despite remaining aware of these, you are still vividly reliving a past life. Sounds and smells from your present life do not interfere with reliving a past life. In fact, it's good that you remain aware of everything that's going on. If an emergency occurred in your present life, you'd instantly return to your current life and be able to deal with it.

Other Methods of Retrieving Past-Life Memories

There are many other techniques that can be used to retrieve memories of your past lives.[10] You can dowse for your past lives, you can use astrology and numerology to provide insight into your past lives, you can meditate, and you can even experience dreams about your past lives. You can also use your memory to go back before your birth in this lifetime. This is known as "far memory."

Far memory and dreaming are the only methods, apart from hypnosis, that allow you to relive experiences from your past lives. Because of that, we'll discuss them briefly here.

Far Memory

An elderly friend named Stephen taught me this technique more than thirty years ago. Stephen suffered from insomnia and filled in the hours waiting for sleep to come by thinking about different experiences he'd had. He tried to remember every detail of every experience. Over a period of time, he went further and further into his past until he was reliving experiences from his early childhood.

He was brought up in the east end of London and remembered being taken out shopping with his mother. Stephen discovered that, with practice, he was able to recall the name of every shop on the street. In fact, in his mind's eye he was able to "see" the entire street and all the shops exactly as they were when he was a small boy.

Stephen decided to go back even further, and recalled an incident when he was one year old and his mother rushed him to the hospital. He was fascinated to discover that he had memories dating back that far, and tried to go back even further.

After experiencing feelings of comfort and security, which made him think he'd returned to the womb, Stephen suddenly saw himself as an adult again. As he knew nothing about reincarnation, this experience terrified him, and he returned to the present.

A few nights later, Stephen decided to see what would happen if he tried again. He took himself back to the womb, and suddenly found himself as a young man hiding in a swamp while men and dogs searched for him. They failed to find his hiding place, but the young man froze to death during the night.

Stephen became obsessed with this young man, and tried to learn more about him every night. He had planned to write a book about his earlier life but unfortunately died before he could do so. Stephen was initially reluctant to accept that he was reliving a past life. I encouraged him to go back even further, but he refused to do so, as he was so fascinated with the lifetime he had uncovered.

Far memory is a deceptively easy way to experience past lives. However, most people find that it takes a great deal of practice to achieve success. My friend Stephen spent months reliving experiences from his current life before he suddenly found himself in a past life. Consequently, it is a good idea to have several sessions to see how far back you can go in this lifetime before trying to return to a past life.

Stephen suffered from insomnia, which is why he could do this lying in bed. Whenever I've tried to do this in bed at night, I've fallen asleep before returning to a past life. Consequently, I usually relax in a comfortable chair, or lie on the floor, when doing this. In the summer months, I enjoy doing this experiment outdoors. However, I've met many people who are able to do this in bed before falling asleep. They are extremely fortunate, as they can easily fall asleep afterwards no matter what the outcome is.

Once you're comfortable, start by taking several deep breaths and relaxing as much as you can. Visualize an important event that occurred within the last few years. As people see things in different ways, you may see the event clearly in your mind. This means you're a visual person. You may be an auditory person and hear what is occurring as you relive the experience. If you're a kinesthetic person, you'll feel or sense the experience. There is no right or wrong way to visualize an experience.

Once you've relived the event in your mind, let it go, and allow yourself to drift back further to another experience. Continue doing this until you've gone as far back as you can in this lifetime.

At this point, think of your desire to experience one of your past lives, and see if you can go back even further. If you're successful, explore the past life for as long as you wish, and then return to the present. It's more likely, especially on your first few attempts, that you'll either go back to a forgotten incident from your current life or will experience nothing at all.

Patience is required when learning this method. Although the far memory technique sounds easy, most people find it can take months before they achieve success. The most important part of the exercise is to simply relax and allow it to happen.

Lucid Dreaming

A lucid dream occurs when you are in a dream and become aware that you are dreaming. Most people have experienced this sensation. Usually the dream takes over again and the conscious mind returns to sleep. However, it's possible in this situation to direct the dream anywhere you wish using your conscious mind.

Edgar Cayce, the famous American psychic, experienced a lucid dream during World War I. In 1910, his wife had given birth to their second son, but sadly the baby lived for only two months. Some years later, Edgar dreamed that he had met and talked with some of his Sunday school pupils who had been killed during the war. While still dreaming, Edgar thought that as he had been able to see these young soldiers, even though they were dead, there had to be a way to see his son. Instantly he found himself in a room full of babies, one of whom was smiling at him. This was his son. This dream provided consolation for the grieving father, and afterwards Edgar was able to move forward again.[11]

Although virtually everyone has experienced an involuntary lucid dream, it takes practice to be able to have one when you want to. Fortunately, there are a number of things you can do to increase the chances of experiencing a lucid dream.

As you're drifting off to sleep, tell yourself that you will experience a lucid dream. You need to say this to yourself in a casual, nonchalant manner. If you demand a lucid dream, you can almost guarantee that it won't happen. You might say: "Tonight, as I dream, I'll realize I'm dreaming and will immediately go back to an important experience that occurred in a past life."

If you happen to wake up during the night and feel that you're dropping straight back to sleep, again request a lucid dream.

You probably won't experience a lucid dream the first time you try, but if you persevere you'll suddenly find yourself experiencing a past life. You'll be able to move backwards and forwards in this past life. If anything unpleasant occurs, you'll be able to move back and observe what is happening in a detached manner from a distance. You'll also be able to move closer to any event, if you wish. While you're experiencing this past life, try to discover what your main purpose was in this incarnation. Experience situations that enable you to spend time with the people who were closest to you, and also find out what you enjoyed doing most.

You can return to the present any time you wish while you're lucid dreaming. Although you may be experiencing a lifetime that occurred hundreds or even thousands of years ago, you remain aware that you are lucid dreaming. Once you've experienced enough of the past life, you can return to the present and drift back to sleep.

When you wake up in the morning, record everything you can remember about your past life. You can gain further information by returning to that past life as many times as you wish. Over a period of time, you'll build up a valuable record of many of your past lives.

The common factor in all of your past lives is your soul. Although your physical body dies and decays, your soul continues to learn and grow as it experiences incarnation after incarnation. We'll look at the soul in the next chapter.

CHAPTER TWO

WHAT IS THE SOUL?

IN HIS ACCEPTANCE SPEECH, Nobel Prize winner William Faulkner (1897–1962) said:

> I believe man will not merely endure, he will prevail. He is immortal, not because he, alone among creatures, has an inexhaustible voice but because he has a soul, a spirit capable of compassion and sacrifice and endurance.[1]

Faulkner obviously had a strong belief in the soul and knew that it provided humankind with many positive qualities, such as compassion, sacrifice, and endurance. However, powerful though his words are, they do not define the soul.

The soul is often described as the spiritual and immortal part of a human being. It is a distinct entity that is separate from the physical body. The soul is the person's essential essence. It is the animating principle that enables the physical body to live. It is also the person's life force, the seat of his or her personality, and the spark of the Divine that is found within each cell of the body. The soul is eternal. It existed before the person was born and continues to exist after he or she dies. The personality is the part that is born and ultimately dies, but the soul is immortal. The soul is your connection to the ultimate life force. Unfortunately, the word *soul* is also frequently used as a synonym for *mind* or *self*.

In his book *Wisdom of the Ages*, Dr. Wayne W. Dyer writes: "Your soul has no boundaries, no form, no dimensions to measure. Yet it is the very core of your being. When you are able to experience that space, you will know the peace and joy that comes from a life fully lived and fully appreciated."[2]

Belief in the soul has been a common phenomenon throughout the world for thousands of years, even though people have struggled to define it. The soul is often considered to be an invisible substance that is present in people who are alive but absent in people who have died. Many people also believe that the soul can temporarily leave the body, especially when the person is asleep. Memories of dreams in which someone traveled widely, yet woke up safely in bed, are probably the reason behind this belief. In their minds, the person's soul made the trip, while his or her physical body remained asleep, and temporarily soulless, in bed.

It is not simply good manners to cover your mouth when yawning. In the past, people believed that when someone died, the soul left the body with the person's final breath. Consequently, covering the mouth when yawning prevented the soul from accidentally leaving the body prematurely.

The English poet John Keats (1795–1821) had a keen interest in philosophy and believed everyone was born with "sparks of the divinity." However, these did not become souls until the person acquired an identity. Keats wrote about this in a letter to his brother and sister, George and Georgiana, on February 14, 1819:

Call the world if you please "The vale of Soul-making" ... I say "Soul making" Soul as distinguished from an Intelligence—There may be intelligences or sparks of the divinity in millions—but they are not Souls till they acquire identities, till each one is personally itself. I[n]telligences are atoms of perception—they know and they see and they are pure, in short they are God—How then are Souls to be made? ... This is effected by three grand materials acting the one upon the other for a series of years. These three Materials are the Intelligence—the human heart (as distinguished from intelligence or Mind) and the World or Elemental space suited for the proper action of Mind and Heart on each other for the purpose of forming the Soul or Intelligence destined to possess the sense of Identity.[3]

Ralph Waldo Emerson (1803–1882) wrote in his *Journals:*

The soul is an emanation of the Divinity, a part of the soul of the world, a ray from the source of light. It comes from without into the human body, as into a temporary abode, it goes out of it anew; it wanders in ethereal regions, it returns to visit it ... it passes into other habitations, for the soul is immortal.[4]

These definitions of the soul might sound rather technical. However, the reality is quite different, and I'm sure you've seen the souls of other people at different times in your life. Whenever you see someone totally lost in an awe-inspiring, magical, or tender moment, you'll see his or her soul. You'll see the person in a completely different, almost incandescent way. Here's an example.

My daughter, Charlotte, married her longtime boyfriend, Jeff, about twelve years ago. They chose to get married at a beautiful vineyard on a beautiful island that offered magnificent views back to the mainland, where they lived. It was a gorgeous, sunny afternoon, and after the wedding the bridal couple went down to a beach for the wedding photographs. As Charlotte turned to look at Jeff, I saw an emanation of light completely surrounding her. It was so magnificent it brought tears to my eyes. When I could see properly again, the moment had passed, and Charlotte was her normal self again.

I have seen this on other occasions, too. My sister is involved with a group called Riding for the Disabled. They use horses to increase the confidence of people with physical or intellectual difficulties. On one occasion I was there when a small, physically disabled boy was placed on a horse. He was terrified for the first few seconds, but gradually became used to the sensation of sitting on a large animal. After a few minutes, one of the helpers led the horse around a quarter-mile circuit. When they returned, the boy was ecstatic. He had a huge grin on his face, and light shone from every cell of his body.

As these moments come and go in a matter of seconds, they can easily be missed. However, when you happen to see one, it becomes an experience you'll remember for the rest of your life.

The Christian View of the Soul

The term *immortal soul* appears nowhere in the New Testament or in the writings of early Christian theologians. This is because early Christians followed the Jewish belief that union with God meant a union involving the whole person, and this meant both body and soul.[5] They believed that the body and the soul were separate entities.

Gradually, over a period of time, the Christian church came to accept two apparently opposing ideas: the resurrection of the body as well as the immortality of the soul. St.

Paul must have been thinking about this when he wrote, "There is a natural body, and there is a spiritual body" (1 Corinthians 15:44). He was also writing for any of his readers who may have been influenced by the Gnostics.

For the first two hundred years of its existence, Christianity was divided into two main groups. Christian Gnosticism was influenced by Judaism, Persian teachings, and Platonist philosophy. The Gnostics believed in dualism, as they accepted the Devil as a deity who was opposed to God. They considered the body to be unclean and a prison for the soul. In their teachings, the soul is liberated at death and ascends heavenwards to become reunited with God.

Orthodox Christians opposed the Gnostic teachings, as they believed in monism (one God) and the resurrection of the body. They did not accept that the soul had existed before someone was born, or that it reincarnated into another body after the person's death.

In the third century CE, Greek philosophical ideas about the superiority of the soul began playing a role in theological thought. Influenced more by Plato than Aristotle, the Christian fathers started teaching the concept that the soul survived even though the physical body died.

Origen (c. 185–c. 254), a prolific writer and biblical scholar, believed the soul was immortal, and existed before the current lifetime and survived the person's physical death. However, this was an exceptional point of view. St. Augustine (354–430) suggested a more limited view of the soul. He wrote that the soul mirrored the Trinity, as it contained the three qualities of memory, understanding, and will. However, like the physical body, the soul was created by God, and could not exist without Him.

St. Thomas Aquinas (1225–1274) thought that God made each soul expressly for a specific body, but that it could live independently from the body, as the soul survived from the time of the person's death until his or her resurrection.

St. Teresa of Ávila (1515–1582) had an extremely clear image of the soul. She wrote: "I began to think of the soul as if it were a castle made of a single diamond or of very clear crystal, in which there are many rooms, just as in heaven there are many mansions... some above, others below, others at each side; and in the center and midst of them all is the chiefest mansion where the most secret things pass between God and the soul."[6]

Many Christians believe in a soul-body dualism. Humans are made in the image of God, and the soul is a gift from God. In 1869, the Roman Catholic Church declared that the soul is present at the moment of conception. Many people, especially Roman Catholics, believe this today. Ralph McInerny, the Michael P. Grace Professor of Medieval Studies at the University of Notre Dame and an eminent Catholic scholar, wrote: "A soul is not produced from matter but breathed into the conceptum by God."[7] Today, a more common Christian point of view is to consider people as spiritual beings who have gradually developed both subjectivity and self-transcendence.

The Jewish View of the Soul

Jewish people consider the body and the soul to be united. After death, the soul goes to Gehenna to be cleansed and purified. This can take, in extreme cases, up to eleven months. This is why Jewish people recite the kaddish, a prayer of memory, for eleven months after a parent dies.

In the first century CE, the Jewish soldier and historian Flavius Josephus (c. 37–?) wrote that the Essenes, an ascetic Jewish sect, believed that the soul was preexistent and immortal. He also wrote that the Pharisees believed the souls of evil people were punished after death. However, the souls of good people were reincarnated into other bodies. As there is no evidence that Jewish people believed in reincarnation, it's possible that Josephus meant "resurrection" rather than "reincarnation."

The Talmud, a compilation of rabbinical thought, dates back to about the fourth century CE. It discusses *gilgul neshamot*, which means "the judgment of the revolutions of the souls." In the revolutions of the souls, people who had been particularly evil had the opportunity to reincarnate and lead worthwhile lives. Moses and Jethro, for instance, were believed to be the gilgulim (reincarnations) of Cain and Abel.

In the seventeenth century, Rabbi Menasseh ben Israel (1604–1657) wrote *Nishmat Hayyim (The Soul of Life)*, in which he claimed that "the belief or the doctrine of the transmigration of souls is a firm and infallible dogma accepted by the whole assemblage of our church."[8]

Today, Orthodox Jews believe in the resurrection. However, many non-Orthodox Jews believe that we possess immortal souls.

The Islamic View of the Soul

In Islam, there are two Arabic words for the soul. The first of these is *nafs,* which means "the independent soul." It equates to the Greek word *psyche.* Nafs sometimes represents the unperfected soul that needs to be nurtured and guided until it becomes a soul at peace. The other Arabic word for soul is *ruh,* which means "spirit," or "the non-independent soul." Ruh is synonymous with the Greek word *nous.* Ruh is the central part of a human being and contains the spirit of God.

Nafs and ruh are, respectively, the lower and higher, or the human and divine, levels of the soul.

The Hindu View of the Soul

The nearest Hindu equivalent to the soul is *atman*, which is the person's real self. The word atman originally meant "breath," but it now has a wide range of meanings taught by different branches of Hinduism.

The Upanishads discuss *paramatman*, or universal soul. This is identical to the individual atmans, which ultimately merge with it. This concept is known as *nirguna brahman,* which means an absolute reality that is impersonal and free from all human qualities. The individual atmans remain in limbo for a period of time and then reincarnate into another person. They continue reincarnating until the atman, or soul, becomes perfect and becomes one with Brahman (the Divine). This is called *moksha* and is the ultimate goal of all Hindus.

The Bhagavad Gita, the sacred Hindu text, says: "Just as a man discards worn out clothes and puts on new clothes, the soul discards worn out bodies and wears new ones" (2:22).

The Buddhist View of the Soul

Buddhists believe in reincarnation and karma. They believe that the soul will be born again, and that it will carry with it all the karma and lessons it has learned from previous incarnations. They believe that by following the teachings of Buddha in this life, they will progress in their next incarnation.

Buddhists and Hindus share the doctrine of *samsara*. This is the cycle of birth, death, and rebirth that continues until the person is liberated from it. However, there is an important difference between the two religions. Hindus believe that humans possess a changeless soul, which transmigrates from person to person during different incarnations. Buddhists believe that everything is impermanent. This means the soul is also impermanent, and cannot be fixed and unchangeable. Buddha rejected the idea of an immortal soul, as he considered it to be, like God, wishful thinking created by people who sought immortality.[9]

The Tibetan Book of the Dead explains the *bardos*, or the space between lives, that the consciousness of the deceased person must experience before being born again. Bardos usually last forty-nine days. During the first twenty-one days the soul is dealing with the karma from the lifetime that has just ended, and in the remaining twenty-eight days it is working toward its rebirth. Buddhists believe that the person's consciousness is extremely clairvoyant during its bardo state, and consequently family and friends of the deceased think about, pray for, and send best wishes to the deceased person at this time, as they believe it will help him or her make a positive rebirth. In Tibet, family members also read *The Tibetan Book of the Dead* out loud to help provide guidance to the person's consciousness while it is in the bardo state.

The Chinese View of the Soul

In China, the Taoists and Confucians believe in two kinds of soul, known as the *hun* and the *po*. Varying sources claim that humans have different numbers of hun and po souls. However, everyone has at least one hun soul and one po soul. The hun soul is made up of yang energy and looks after the person's spiritual and intellectual aspects, while the hun comprises yin energy, which provides life to the body. When the person dies, the souls leave the body. The hun souls ascend, and the po souls sink into the person's grave. Special rituals are performed to encourage the hun souls to move into the family's ancestral tablets. The same rituals ensure the po souls remain peacefully in the grave with the body.

As well as becoming used to their new homes in the grave, the po souls also descend into the Chinese version of hell, where their deeds are judged by the Ten Magistrates who preside over the Ten Tribunals. Each tribunal tries different types of offenses. The magistrates are appointed by Yama, the king of hell. What happens next depends on the person's karma (good deeds compared with bad deeds). There are a number of punishment levels in hell, and the soul spends enough time in each of these to balance its karma before reaching the final court to make sure the soul has fully atoned for its actions. Only then can it be reincarnated into another body.

Multiple Souls

The ancient Egyptians believed that they had seven souls given to them at birth by the Seven Hathors, the goddesses of fate. The Hathors, usually depicted as seven beautiful women, were present at every birth and predicted the baby's destiny. The Hathors were sometimes depicted as seven cows, but they appeared in this form mainly at funerals accompanied by the Sky Bull. The Hathors were called upon for help in matters concerning love and protection from evil. The Seven Hathors also protected the heavenly spheres in the sky.

The seven Egyptian souls are:[10]

   1. aakhu: the life spirit, located in the blood.

   2. ab: the heart, created from the heart blood of the person's mother.

3. **ba:** a birdlike ghost that appeared after death and flew into and out of the person's grave.

4. **ka:** the person's reflection.

5. **khaibut:** the person's shadow.

6. **khat:** the person's physical body.

7. **ren:** the person's secret soul-name.

The poet and mystic Gerald Massey (1828–1907) wrote and lectured on the subject of seven souls and noted the similarities between the systems of seven souls developed in India and Egypt. Here are his versions of the seven souls.[11] Note that his version of the Egyptian souls is slightly different from the one just given.

Indian

1. **rupa:** the body, or element of form.

2. **prana, or jiva:** the breath of life.

3. **astral:** body.

4. **manus:** intelligence.

5. **khama-rupa:** animal soul.

6. **buddhi:** spiritual soul.

7. **atma:** pure spirit.

Egyptian

1. **kha:** body.

2. **ba:** the soul of breath.

3. khabs: the shade.

4. akhu: intelligence or perception.

5. seb: ancestral soul.

6. putah: the first intellectual father.

7. atmu: divine, or eternal, soul.

Gnostic Christianity adopted the Egyptian concept of seven souls, and reduced it to a single soul that was modified and influenced by the seven known planets as it passed through each of them in turn on its journey from heaven to the body of a newly born baby. Consequently, the purity of the soul was weakened as it learned the seven deadly sins. Fortunately, this situation was reversed when the soul left the body after death and returned to heaven. Although most Christians accepted the concept of a single soul, some Gnostics believed that everyone possessed two souls: one from the person's mind and the other from God.

Members of the Menomini tribe of American Indians believe that the head and the heart each contain a soul. The Bagobo people in the Philippines believe there is one soul for the left side of the body and another soul for the right. After death, one of these souls joins its ancestors, while the other becomes a ghost.

Some concepts of multiple souls appear strange to outsiders. The Jívaro people of Ecuador believe that everyone has three souls. The first is a soul you have from birth, called *wakani*. When you die, this soul returns to the place where you were born and turns into a demon. The demon then dies and transforms into a giant moth, which becomes a fine mist when it dies. The second soul is called *arutam*. You can gain this soul by fasting, bathing under a waterfall, and imbibing a hallucinogenic juice. Unfortunately, this soul makes you feel capable of doing anything but temporarily leaves you when it is really needed. The third soul is an avenging soul, known as *muisak*. This soul attempts to leave the head of anyone who has been murdered so it can avenge the person's death. Consequently, if you kill someone, it is important to shrink that person's head.[12]

In Indian mysticism there are three main bodies: the physical, the astral, and the causal. Naturally, everyone is aware of the physical body, but few people are aware of their astral and causal bodies. The astral body is the same form as the physical body, but is composed of a form of subtle matter known as prana. The causal body is egg-shaped and is a body of light. These three bodies can be related to the body, mind, and soul.

The Causal Body

In Hindu mysticism, the causal body is considered to be the body of the soul. In the nineteenth century, the Theosophical Society introduced this concept to the Western world, and today it is accepted by many people interested in New Age concepts.

The causal body contains everything you have experienced and learned in previous incarnations. It is where your consciousness comes from. It provides the divine spark that gives you life. It also provides you with your personality. When your life ends, your personality returns to the causal body and adds its love and knowledge to everything that was learned in earlier lifetimes.

As the person evolves spiritually, the causal body contacts other souls who are at the same level. They are able to communicate with each other without the assistance of the human bodies that are their temporary homes in this lifetime. By doing this, the causal body helps the person develop positive qualities, such as love, unity, wisdom, and a sense of purpose.

Soul Awareness Exercise

Many years ago, a friend of mine experienced a dramatic change in his life. He was a successful businessman, but his endless pursuit of money and possessions had brought him little pleasure or satisfaction. Eventually he started thinking, *There must be more to life than this.* We had a number of discussions about better ways of living, and he became interested in the concept of the soul.

"Something is missing in my life," he told me. "I don't even know what it is, but I've a deep longing for it. Is it possible that I'm missing my soul?"

Of course, he wasn't missing a soul, but he did need to learn how to connect with it. He'd spent most of his life living through his head, but next to no time connecting with his heart. People who live in their heads always find it hard to connect with their soul, as they try to make the connection intellectually. Fortunately, once my friend became aware of his divine soul, and experienced it, he was able to progress again, but as a markedly different man. He is still successful in business, but is now equally well known as a philanthropist. This is the exercise I taught him.

You can do this exercise whenever you wish to connect with your soul. If you are familiar with relaxation techniques, you'll be able to contact your soul in a matter of seconds. If you have not yet learned how to relax quickly, you should allow about thirty minutes to complete the exercise. With practice, you'll find it easier and easier to relax completely and will be able to perform this exercise in a matter of minutes.

You should wear comfortable, loose-fitting clothing. Make sure the room is pleasantly warm but not hot. Temporarily disconnect the phone so you won't be disturbed or interrupted while you are doing the exercise.

You can sit in a comfortable recliner chair, or lie down on a bed or the floor. I prefer lying on the floor, as I tend to go to sleep when doing this exercise on a bed. Cover yourself with a blanket, because you're likely to lose a couple of degrees of body heat while doing the exercise.

Make yourself as comfortable as you can. When you feel ready, close your eyes and take ten slow, deep breaths. Hold each inhalation of breath for a couple of seconds before exhaling. Each time you exhale, say to yourself, "Relax, relax, relax."

Once you've completed the ten deep breaths, forget about your breathing and allow your attention to focus on the toes of your left foot. Allow these toes to relax as much as possible. You might feel a slight tingling sensation in your toes as you do this. When you feel your toes have relaxed, allow the relaxation to spread into your left foot, and up to your ankle.

Take as long as necessary to make sure your left foot is totally relaxed, and then repeat this with the toes of your right foot. Once these toes are relaxed, allow the relaxation to drift into your right foot, up to the ankle.

Both feet should be completely relaxed now. Allow the relaxation to drift up one leg. Imagine it relaxing every cell as it slowly moves up your leg, relaxing your calf, knee, and thigh. When one leg feels totally relaxed, allow the relaxation to drift up the other leg.

Allow the relaxation to drift up your abdomen, into your stomach and up to your chest. Let your shoulders relax, and then let the pleasant relaxation drift down one arm to the tips of your fingers. Repeat with the other arm.

When you feel both arms are relaxed, focus on your neck, and allow all the muscles in your neck to relax. Gradually allow the relaxation to drift up into your face. Pay special attention to the muscles around your eyes. These are the finest muscles in your whole body. Once these muscles are completely relaxed, allow the relaxation to drift up to the top of your head.

You are now completely relaxed. Mentally scan your body to make sure this is the case. Focus on any areas that do not feel totally relaxed, and allow all the muscles in the area to dissolve and relax.

Take another three slow, deep breaths, and then visualize yourself in the most peaceful and beautiful setting you can imagine. People visualize in different ways. Some people are able to clearly "see" the scene in their imagination. Others "see" it faintly. Others experience the scene in different ways. They might feel a pleasant warmth, hear sounds, or simply know they're in a comfortable, tranquil paradise created by their imagination.

Allow yourself to become familiar with the situation and the magnificent surroundings you find yourself in. You might feel the pleasant sunlight on your body. You might hear the sounds of birds or the lapping of waves on a beach. You'll certainly find yourself relaxing even more as you go deeper and deeper into your own special, personal paradise.

Notice how calm and relaxed you feel. See yourself as the wonderful creation you are. You are special. You are important. You are a vital, integral part of the universe. You have a right to be happy, to experience all the good things life has to offer. As you relax even further, become aware that this special, secret, magical world has been created by your soul. You are basking in the rich, protective glow of your soul.

Allow yourself to feel this with every breath you take, as you drift even deeper into complete and total relaxation. Feel the beautiful, comforting warmth all around you, and feel appreciated, loved, and nurtured by your soul. Allow this energizing warmth to nurture and heal every part of your mind, body, and soul.

As you're relaxing in the magical kingdom of your soul, allow yourself to receive all the love the universe is willingly giving you. Accept this love, because you deserve it. You deserve nothing but the best. When you feel completely full of love, allow it to spill over and spread throughout your magical world and out to the room you're lying in. Once the room is full of love, allow it to spread throughout the building and continue to spread on and on, until the whole world is full of your love.

Bask in this love for as long as you wish. See yourself as a happy, loving, confident, strong, powerful, generous, protective, and loving person. Your immortal soul has created this magical world purely for you, and you can return here as often as you wish. Whenever you want to feel loved, appreciated, and blessed, all you need do is relax and return to your own special world.

Remain in this special place for as long as you wish. When you feel ready to return to your everyday world, take five slow, deep breaths, mentally counting from one to five. When you reach five, open your eyes, become familiar with the situation around you, stretch, and relax for a few moments before getting up. If you're doing this exercise in bed at night, you can remain in your pleasant paradise until you drift off to sleep.

Some people find it easy to relax, but others find it difficult. Even if you find it easy to relax, it's a good idea to go through the complete relaxation process before visualizing your personal paradise, for at least the first three or four times. Once you've become used to the procedure, you'll be able to use whatever method you wish to relax.

If you find it difficult to relax, you'll find this exercise a useful way to learn progressive relaxation. With practice, it will gradually become easier and easier to relax. In time, you'll find you'll be able to spend most of your time inside your personal paradise rather than on the process of relaxing your physical body.

Layers of the Soul

The soul is present in every cell of the human body. This must be the case, as the soul animates every part of the body. However, the soul is also a spirit, which means it has no form and cannot be located and identified like any of the other essential organs of the body. It may well exist outside the physical body.

Alvin Plantinga, the John A. O'Brien Professor of Philosophy at the University of Notre Dame, believes this is the case. He demonstrates the existence of the soul in an interesting way. He argues that if every part of his body was immediately replaced by other body parts while he remained conscious, and the original body parts were destroyed, he would continue to exist, even though his original body had ceased to exist. Consequently, the soul exists separately from the physical body.[13]

If this is the case, where is the soul located? The most logical place is in the subtle body, the invisible electromagnetic energy field, or aura, that surrounds all living things. We'll look at the aura more closely in the next chapter.

CHAPTER THREE

YOU ARE
A RAINBOW

MOST PEOPLE ARE UNAWARE that their physical body is just one of several bodies they possess. This is because it usually takes time and effort to learn how to see the other bodies. This is unfortunate, as people's lives would change overnight if they could see the potential that is visible in their aura.

I know a young man who disassociated himself from his former friends after developing the ability to see auras. "They were all losers," he told me. "And I'd have been a loser, too, if I'd stayed with them. We were doing drugs and other things. My life changed once I started seeing auras and discovered how incredible everyone is. Most people have no idea how great their potential is. Once I saw that I could achieve virtually anything, it seemed almost criminal not to act on it."

This former high-school dropout is now in his third year of college.

Dictionaries describe the aura as an electromagnetic energy field that surrounds all living things. The word aura is derived from the Greek word *avra,* which means "air" or "a breeze." It is often described as an egg-shaped ball of energy that surrounds the body. Ursula Roberts, the British medium and author, described the aura as "a magnetic field of vibration which surrounds every person, in the same way that light surrounds a lighted candle or perfume surrounds a flower."[1] This is only partially correct. As the aura is part of every cell in the body, it is an extension of the body that in an average person extends for eight to ten feet in all directions. Some highly spiritual people have extremely large auras that are said to extend for several miles. Gautama Buddha's early followers claimed his aura extended two hundred miles.[2]

The aura expands and contracts in size depending on the health, vitality, and mental state of the person. Someone who is reasonably fit and full of the joys of life will have a much larger aura than someone who is unwell or has a negative outlook on life. The person with the larger aura will feel more in control of his or her life than the person with the smaller aura.

Anxiety, stress, frustration, anger, hostility, low self-esteem, and poor social skills weaken the aura. Friends, a loving family, happiness, humanitarian ideals, love, hobbies, and enjoyable work all strengthen the aura.

Your aura constantly interacts with the auras of others. Consequently, your aura expands and contracts as you go through each day. It expands when you meet positive people and contracts when you spend time with negative people.

It is also affected by encounters with people you like and dislike. Like everyone else, you absorb and pass out aura energy everywhere you go. This is why you feel depleted and drained of energy after spending time with negative people. Fortunately, this works the other way, too, and you feel invigorated and restored after spending time with positive people.

Anticipation also affects the size of the aura. Someone who is waiting to meet his or her lover will have a large, expansive aura, while someone expecting a rebuke or set-back will have a small aura.

Auras contain all the colors of the rainbow. Auras also change color to reveal people's moods and emotions. Someone who is "in the pink" is likely to be happier than someone who is "green with envy" or "red with rage." Someone in a "black hole" is depressed, while a coward is said to be "yellow." All of these expressions came into being because people noticed these colors in people's auras and discovered they consistently described the person's emotional state.

Even if you haven't yet seen an aura, you'll have been affected by other people's life force energy from the moment you were born. Recently, my wife and I met a friend while we were walking along a beach. He called out a cheery hello and joined us for a few minutes. After he left, my wife said, "He's such a nice man. He radiates charm." On the same walk, she described someone else as "glowing with happiness." In both instances, my wife was describing the person's aura.

People have been interested in the aura for thousands of years. There are at least three passages in the Bible that appear to relate to auras.[3] In the Beatitudes, Jesus taught something that appears to relate to auras: "Let your light so shine before men, that they may see your good works" (Matthew 5:16). The halos that Christian artists draw around Jesus Christ, the apostles, saints, martyrs, and angels are their depictions of auras that show their spiritually evolved state. It's interesting to note that artists in ancient Egypt, Greece, Rome, and India also used halos to illustrate this well before Christian times.

The aura provides a clear picture of the person's character, emotional state, attitude, values, habitual thoughts, health, vitality, and mood. It reveals his or her physical, mental, emotional, and spiritual energy. Positive and negative experiences from the past are shown in the aura. It also reveals the soul's journey through many past incarnations to the present. People who see auras are often able to detect illnesses in the aura well before they become apparent in the physical body.

Layers of the Aura

The aura consists of a number of layers known as *subtle bodies*. In the East, these layers are known as *koshas*, or "sheaths." This is a good name, as people who are able to see the aura often remark that the layers look like sheaths.

Most people, with practice, are able to feel three layers (the etheric double, the astral body, and the mental body), but many highly intuitive people can feel a number of other layers, even if they can't see them.

Many clairvoyants can feel seven layers of the aura (figure 1):

1. The physical etheric plane

2. The astral (or emotional) plane

3. The lower mental plane

4. The higher mental plane

5. The spiritual plane

6. The intuitional plane

7. The absolute plane

These seven layers relate to the seven chakras, which we'll discuss in the next chapter. In the past, the seven layers of the aura were looked at individually. The astral plane related to emotions, for instance, while the mental bodies related to thought. However, thoughts affect our emotions, and emotions affect our thoughts. Consequently, today most people look at the aura as a whole.

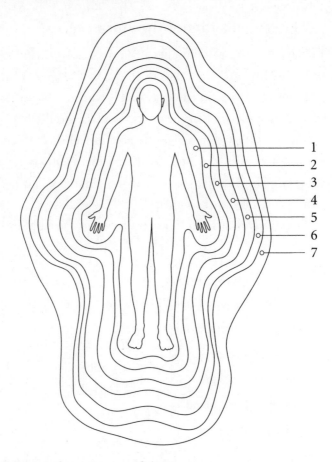

Figure 1: Seven Layers of the Aura

    1. The physical plane (etheric double)

    2. The astral (or emotional) plane

    3. The lower mental plane

    4. The higher mental plane

    5. The spiritual plane

    6. The intuitional plane

    7. The absolute plane

Although the layers of the aura can be felt individually, the aura as a whole appears to be a gridlike matrix of swirling energy, in which all the layers mix and interact with each other.

The Physical Plane (Etheric Double)

The physical plane, or etheric double, is a fine, almost invisible layer that extends between a quarter inch and half an inch around the body. The etheric double appears to be a type of battery that recharges itself when the person is asleep. This is because it expands during sleep and contracts during the waking hours.

When people first start seeing auras, they see the etheric double as a clear space between the physical body and the aura. However, as their skills develop, they notice that the etheric double has a grayish tinge that is constantly shimmering and moving. This movement creates a variety of delicate, almost luminous, constantly changing colors that range from white to blue.

The etheric double is often called the health aura, as ill health is revealed as a dark smudge or a break in the movements inside the etheric double. Illnesses can often be detected in the etheric double long before the person realizes something is wrong. Medical intuitives who examine the etheric double can see past health problems as well as present and future concerns inside this layer.

You can also see someone's basic nature in the etheric double. Someone who constantly thinks negative thoughts has a dull etheric double, especially when compared to the beautiful, bright, and radiant etheric double that belongs to someone who looks mainly on the bright side of life.

The Astral Plane

The astral plane, sometimes called the emotional layer, relates to feelings, emotions, and desires. It is sometimes referred to as the "animal soul," as it is concerned with the person's subconscious mind. All the person's emotional experiences, good and bad, are stored here.

The Lower Mental Plane

The lower mental plane relates to reason, thought, ideas, and the conscious mind. This is where most people spend their waking hours. The lower mental plane expands when the person is involved in study or deep thought. The person's beliefs, values, and ideals are stored here.

The Higher Mental Plane

The higher mental plane, sometimes known as the causal plane, relates to the higher mind, love for self and others, and unconditional love. The higher mental plane connects the lower mental plane (conscious mind) to the spiritual plane.

The Spiritual Plane

The spiritual plane, sometimes known as the etheric plane, is the home of the person's spirituality. It connects the person with the universe.

The prophet Ezekiel described the spiritual plane as a throne: "Over their heads was the likeness of a throne, as the appearance of a sapphire stone: and upon the likeness of the throne was the likeness as the appearance of a man above upon it. And I saw as the color of amber, as the appearance of fire round about within it, from the appearance of his loins even upward, and from the appearance of his loins even downward, I saw as it were the appearance of fire, and it had brightness round about. As the appearance of the bow that is in the cloud in the day of rain, so was the appearance of the brightness round about" (Ezekiel 1:26–28).

The Intuitional Plane

The intuitional plane, sometimes known as the celestial plane, relates to the person's dreams, intuitions, and spiritual awareness. Every connection ever made to the universal life force is visible here. This plane also relates to forgiveness and acceptance.

The Absolute Plane

The absolute plane, sometimes known as the ketheric plane, balances and harmonizes all the other layers. It contains all the experiences of the person's soul. It connects the person with the universal life force. It also contains a blueprint of the person's spiritual development and potential.

Other Layers of the Aura

When I was living in India, a guru told me the aura consisted of eighty-nine layers. I was impressed, until other gurus gave me different numbers. Most said there were between seven and ten layers. As it's unusual to find people who can feel more than three layers, it's impossible to say how many layers there might be. The names given to the other layers vary enormously, too. These include the soul layer, memory layer, eternal layer, and universal layer.

The Seven Rays

The seven rays have been discussed and written about for more than two thousand years.[4] They are not part of the aura. They are universal energies that, according to ancient esoteric teachings, are expressed by the universal life force and have a profound effect and influence on the soul. Each ray has its own particular energy that produces one of seven different types of souls. Theosophists, members of the Theosophical Society, the worldwide organization formed by Madame Blavatsky in 1876, believe that everything in the entire solar system belongs to one of the seven rays. Alice A. Bailey (1880–1949), the American occultist and founder of the Arcane School, wrote: "Each vibrating unit of energy can say: I am part of a divine whole, which in its septenary [sevenfold] nature expresses to love and life of the One Reality, coloured by one of the seven qualities of love of Deity and responsive to other qualities."[5]

The seven rays were little known in the West until the nineteenth century. Once the Theosophical Society started teaching the principles of the seven rays, knowledge of them spread quickly.

Theosophists associate these rays with the seven spiritual masters (also known as *chohans*, or Lords of the Rays) of the Great White Brotherhood. According to Theosophical lore, these masters secretly govern the world, and encourage its spiritual development.

Theosophists believe the universe is evolving along seven paths, known as rays, and every person is associated with a particular ray. Because of this, the seven rays can be used to determine each person's personality and purpose in life.

Many people believe that every person's soul is attuned to a particular ray to help it achieve its purpose in this incarnation. However, it is more likely that our souls use the energy of one or two particular rays most of the time, but have access to the qualities and energies of the other rays when we need them. Some people naturally use the energies of three or four of the rays, while others, equally as naturally, focus on just one. The particular focus enables the soul to potentially make as much progress as possible in each incarnation.

Here is a description of the seven rays.

First Ray: Ray of Power and Will
Color: Red
Master: El Morya
Gem: Diamond

The first ray is the Ray of Power and Will. It is sometimes called the Ray of Deity, as the purpose of this ray is to confirm the existence of the Divine on a physical level.

This ray provides courage, self-reliance, willpower, and ambition. It gives leadership qualities, a sense of purpose and direction, and the ability to come up with good ideas and make them happen. This ray also provides ultimate wisdom.

Each ray has a negative side to it. Some people on the first ray are arrogant, overly proud, impatient, and domineering. They seek power and will do anything to achieve it. Because of this, negative first ray people are usually egotistical.

Second Ray: Ray of Love-Wisdom
Color: Blue
Master: Kuthumi
Gem: Sapphire

The second ray is the Ray of Love-Wisdom. People on this ray can see themselves from the perspective of the Divine, and this enables kindness, love, and ultimately wisdom to develop. People on this ray are able to send positive and negative feelings and emotions to the Divine for healing and growth.

This ray also provides insight, wisdom, generosity, diplomacy, sympathy, and compassion. People on this ray are empathetic, sensitive, loving, tactful, and tolerant. They are also naturally intuitive and possess healing capabilities.

Most people on the second ray have a positive outlook on life. However, some show the negative qualities of fear, codependency, oversensitivity, indifference, and overprotectiveness. They frequently possess an inferiority complex.

Third Ray: Ray of Active Intelligence

Color: Yellow

Master: Venetian Chohan

Gem: Emerald

The third ray is the Ray of Active Intelligence. This ray enables the Divine to send thoughts and ideas to people on this ray. These people then need to decide whether they will act on them. This ray also enables their decisions, results, and actions to go back to the Divine.

This ray provides creativity, comprehension, understanding, adaptability, and perception. It also gives people on this ray the ability to plan ahead and communicate well with others. People on this ray are good with financial matters and often do well in business. Once they have achieved success, they gain pleasure from using their wealth to help others.

People who operate on the negative side of the third ray are critical, careless with details, manipulative, and devious. They are sometimes absent-minded and find it hard to say no. This can lead to failure, caused by trying to do too many things at once.

Fourth Ray: Ray of Harmony, Beauty, and Art

Color: Green

Master: Serapis

Gem: Jasper

The fourth ray is the Ray of Harmony, Beauty, and Art. This essential harmony usually comes about through conflict. This ray enables the Divine to send people on this ray the heart's desires they need to manifest. It also allows any harmonies or disharmonies to return to the Divine for healing and development.

The fourth ray provides balance, harmony, and stability. It provides inner peace, too, though this usually occurs after a struggle. These people have the ability to captivate and entertain others with various forms of self-expression. They have a good sense of humor and enjoy making people laugh. They have a strong aesthetic sense and enjoy expressing themselves creatively. They possess a strong sense of color, and many utilize this in their careers. Even if it is not being used in this way, their sense of color will be obvious to others. Over a lifetime they develop spiritually, but their faith is always hard won.

The negative qualities of this ray are stress, worry, moodiness, self-absorption, unreliability, indecision, and a lack of confidence. These people usually experience a great deal of turmoil in their lives.

Fifth Ray: Ray of Concrete Knowledge and Science
Color: Orange
Master: Hilarion
Gem: Topaz

The fifth ray is the Ray of Concrete Knowledge and Science. People on this ray have access to knowledge from the past, present, and future, and hopefully make good use of it. This ray also enables them to instill this information into their everyday lives.

The fifth ray provides patience, logic, and the ability to analyze and discern. People on this ray are inventive, precise, and accurate. They enjoy using their brains to analyze, research, and solve complex problems.

The negative aspects of the fifth ray are rigidity, narrow-mindedness, a critical approach, intolerance, overanalysis, and skepticism. These people are usually loners, as they find it hard to fit in and relate well with others.

Sixth Ray: Ray of Devotion and Idealism
Color: Violet
Master: Jesus
Gem: Ruby

The sixth ray is the Ray of Devotion and Idealism. It enters the body as intuition, enabling the Divine to send pure, unconditional love and support to the person. It encourages people on this ray to investigate what is hidden or unknown.

The sixth ray gives enthusiasm, optimism, loyalty, sincerity, humility, and devotion. It gives people on this ray the potential to motivate and inspire others. It also gives them drive and persistence. People on this ray are idealistic and devout.

People operating on the negative side of the sixth ray are impractical, overly emotional, insecure, selfish, and gullible. They are rigid and take everything to extremes.

Seventh Ray: Ray of Order and Ceremonial Magic
Color: Indigo
Master: Comte de Saint-Germain
Gem: Amethyst

The seventh ray is the Ray of Order and Ceremonial Magic. People on this ray have the potential to express themselves effectively, create order out of chaos, and turn their dreams into action. These people also have the qualities of grace, dignity, nobility, and chivalry. They pay attention to detail. They are good organizers and are able to motivate others to achieve worthwhile goals.

People working on the negative side of this ray are materialistic, unoriginal, rigid, and intolerant. They enjoy routine and like to follow the rules. They are often frustrated perfectionists, as perfection is impossible to achieve.

In the next chapter we'll return to the aura and discuss the seven chakras, or energy centers, that are located along the spine.

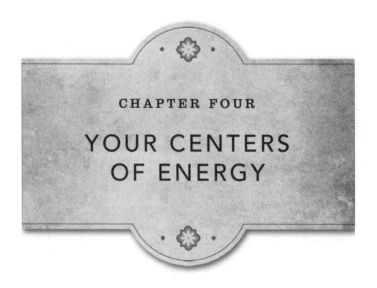

CHAPTER FOUR

YOUR CENTERS OF ENERGY

INSIDE THE AURA, SITUATED in a vertical line in the center of the body in line with the spine, are seven revolving, wheel-like circles of subtle energy called *chakras* (figure 2). The word chakra comes from the Sanskrit word for wheel. In the East, chakras are often depicted as lotus flowers, each with a different number of petals. These petals open and close, reflecting the moods, feelings, and experiences of the person.

The chakras absorb the higher energies, including the universal life force, and transform them into energy that the body can use. They are, in effect, batteries that stimulate the physical and subtle bodies they connect and look after. The universal life force is said to enter the aura through the chakra at the top of the head. It then energizes and stimulates each

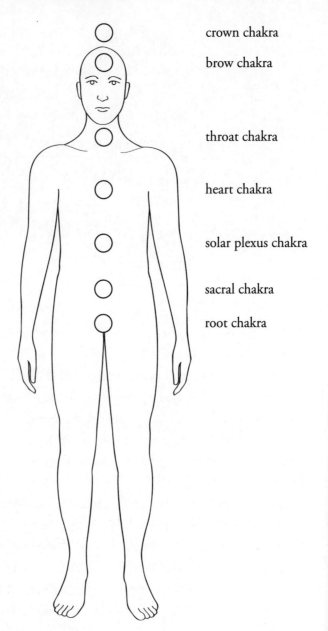

crown chakra

brow chakra

throat chakra

heart chakra

solar plexus chakra

sacral chakra

root chakra

Figure 2: Seven Chakras

chakra as it moves downward through the *nadis*, the channels of energy that connect all the chakras to each other. The word nadi means "flowing water." Six of the chakras are situated on the Sushumna, the main nadi that starts at the base of the spine and ends between the eyebrows at the level of the third eye.

Intertwined with the Sushumna are two other nadis known as Ida and Pingala. They carry the person's male and female energies.

Although most people are not aware of them, the chakras play a vital role in a person's physical, emotional, and mental health. They are powerful batteries that stimulate and energize the entire body.

Each chakra has a number of associations, such as a color, an endocrine gland, and a physical system, along with the organs associated with the system. There is a direct relationship between the state of each chakra and the health of the organs associated with it.

Chakras can be open, closed, in or out of balance, and blocked. All of these conditions affect the chakra. Consequently, if an affected chakra is restored to balance, the person will notice an immediate difference in his or her health, and will experience feelings of well-being. It is unusual to meet someone who has every chakra perfectly balanced. This person would feel contented and be full of all the joys of life. Unfortunately, the fears, worries, frustrations, and stresses of everyday life affect the chakras, which is why it is rare to find someone with all seven chakras in balance.

The concept of chakras is thousands of years old, and a great deal of information about them was recorded in the Upanishads (c. 900–400 BCE), the sacred Hindu texts. Even though the chakras have been utilized in the East for thousands of years, Western science showed no interest in them until the 1970s. The chakra system was little known in the West until the Theosophical Society began teaching it in the late nineteenth century.

The Quatern Chakras

The chakras are frequently depicted as a square and a triangle, known as the *quatern* and the *trinity*. The bottom four chakras represent the quatern. They each represent one of the traditional elements of earth, water, fire, and air.

The quatern chakras have a slower vibration than the three trinity chakras. Because of this, some people feel they are of lesser importance than the chakras in the trinity. This is not the case. Each chakra is essential, as it has its own specific purpose. All of the chakras are equally important.

Root Chakra (Muladhara)
Color: Red
Element: Earth
Functions: Survival, grounding
Glands: Adrenals
Petals: Four
Sense: Smell
Desire: Physical contact

Gemstones: Ruby, garnet, hematite
Challenge: To think before acting
Keyword: Physical

Muladhara is the Sanskrit word for the root chakra. It comes from *mula,* meaning "root," and *adhara,* "support." It is often called the base chakra or support chakra.

The root chakra is situated at the base of the spine in the area of the coccyx. It is concerned with self-preservation and keeps us firmly grounded in the earth. It also provides feelings of security and comfort. It provides vitality, enthusiasm, energy, and a sense of being alive. It symbolizes survival and the life force. Emotionally, it provides drive, courage, strength, and persistence. It also controls our fight-or-flight responses.

The root chakra governs our sense of smell and the solid parts of our body, such as teeth, bones, and nails.

Unlike the other chakras, the root chakra faces downward to the earth.

When the root chakra is understimulated, the person will feel nervous and insecure. This triggers digestive problems and causes fear to gather inside the chakra.

When the root chakra is overstimulated, the person will be self-centered, aggressive, and addicted to money, power, and sex.

When the root chakra is not functioning as it should, the person may suffer from hemorrhoids, constipation, skin irritations, and an increase in weight.

The root chakra can be both calmed and stimulated by meditation. Sit in a straight-backed chair with your feet flat on the floor and your knees creating approximately a ninety-degree angle.

To calm the root chakra, hold a piece of rose quartz behind your back at the base of your spine. Close your eyes, take slow deep breaths, and visualize the gentle, cooling energies of the rose quartz soothing and balancing your root chakra.

To stimulate the root chakra, hold a deep red crystal, such as garnet, at the base of your spine, and visualize its stimulating energy revitalizing, energizing, and balancing your root chakra. You can also stimulate your root chakra by doing anything physical, such as walking, swimming, gardening, or even vacuuming the house.

Sacral Chakra (Svadisthana)

Color: Orange
Element: Water
Functions: Sexuality, creativity, pleasure
Glands: Ovaries, testicles
Petals: Six
Sense: Taste
Desires: Respect and acceptance
Gemstones: Coral, carnelian
Challenge: To love and serve others
Keyword: Social

Svadisthana is the Sanskrit word for the sacral chakra. It means "home of the vital force." This chakra is located at the level of the sacrum in the lower abdomen, approximately two inches below the navel.

Because the sacral chakra is associated with the element of water, it is concerned with all the fluidic functions of the body, including our sense of taste. It represents creativity, sexuality, and emotional balance. It stimulates optimism and hope at an emotional level. People who get along well with others usually have a well-balanced sacral chakra, as this gives them the necessary fluidity to interact with other people easily.

When the sacral chakra is not functioning as it should be, the person may suffer from frigidity or impotence or experience problems with the bladder or kidneys.

The sacral chakra can be both calmed and stimulated by meditation. You can stimulate this chakra by lying on your back on the floor. Bend your knees until you can place the soles of your feet together. Slowly spread your arms until they make a forty-five- to sixty-degree angle to your body. Relax as much as possible, and visualize orange energy filling the area of your sacral chakra until it is overflowing. While remaining in this position, allow yourself to meditate on your sacral chakra for two to three minutes. You can also stimulate your sacral chakra by spending time doing something you enjoy. It can be as simple as meeting a friend for a cup of coffee or taking time out to read an enjoyable book.

You can meditate to soothe and calm your sacral chakra. Sit in a straight-backed chair with your feet flat on the floor and your knees creating approximately a ninety-degree angle. Hold a piece of moonstone to the front of your body below your navel and meditate for a minute or two while the moonstone calms and balances your sacral chakra.

Solar Plexus Chakra (Manipura)

Color: Yellow
Element: Fire
Functions: Will, assertiveness, personal power
Gland: Pancreas
Petals: Ten
Sense: Sight
Desire: To understand
Gemstones: Amber, topaz
Challenge: To communicate effectively with loved ones
Keyword: Intellect

The Sanskrit word Manipura means "jewel of the navel." The solar plexus chakra is located between the navel and the sternum.

The solar plexus chakra provides good self-esteem, warmth, confidence, and happiness. It is involved with the emotions and enhances creativity, optimism, and self-respect at an emotional level. The solar plexus chakra also relates to the eyes.

This chakra can cause anger, resentment, and hostility in people with a negative approach to life. If this chakra is overstimulated, the person will be an overly demanding perfectionist. When the solar plexus chakra is understimulated, the person will be overly sensitive and lacking in confidence.

When the solar plexus chakra is not functioning as it should be, the person may suffer from diabetes, digestive disorders, or hypoglycemia.

The solar plexus chakra can be both calmed and stimulated by meditation. To stimulate this chakra, stand on the floor in bare feet, close your eyes, and visualize your solar plexus chakra completely full with a beautiful yellow energy. Visualize this energy gradually spreading throughout your body. With your eyes remaining closed, start marching slowly on the spot while visualizing your solar plexus chakra becoming revitalized and energized with each movement of your legs. You may find it helpful to make exaggerated movements with your arms and legs while doing this. Stop when you feel that your solar plexus chakra is fully energized. You can also stimulate your solar plexus chakra by setting a worthwhile goal for yourself, and then steadily working at it until it is achieved.

The solar plexus can be soothed and quieted with a piece of quartz crystal. Sit in a straight-backed chair with your feet flat on the floor and your knees creating approximately a ninety-degree angle. Hold the quartz against your solar plexus, close your eyes, and visualize the unwanted energy moving from the chakra into the quartz. Repeat once a day for as long as necessary.

Heart Chakra (Anahatha)

Color: Green
Element: Air
Function: Love
Gland: Thymus
Petals: Twelve
Sense: Touch
Desires: To love and be loved
Gemstones: Emerald, jade, tourmaline
Challenge: To gain confidence
Keyword: Emotions

The heart chakra is located in the center of the chest, in line with the heart. The Sanskrit word Anahatha means "unstruck" or "unbroken." This relates to an eternal sound that has not been created by any human instrument.

The heart chakra relates to personal and unconditional love, sympathy, compassion, understanding, empathy, and the sense of touch.

When the heart chakra is overstimulated, the person will be possessive, controlling, and moody. When the heart chakra is understimulated, the person will feel overly sympathetic and overly sensitive. Most codependent people have an understimulated heart chakra.

When the heart chakra is not functioning as well as it should be, the person may suffer from asthma or have problems with the heart or lungs.

The heart chakra can be both calmed and stimulated by meditation. Sit in a straight-backed chair with your feet flat on the floor and your knees creating an approximately ninety-degree angle. To stimulate your heart chakra, close your eyes and visualize the center of your body in the area of your heart as a glowing green orb. Each time you inhale, allow the orb to grow bigger and bigger until your whole body is inside it. Spend a minute or two enjoying the healing, stimulating energy of the green orb before opening your eyes and carrying on with your day. You also stimulate your heart chakra every time you experience a sense of joy and fulfillment.

To calm your heart chakra, close your eyes and visualize your entire body enveloped in a pure white light. In your imagination, allow the white light to enter your body with each inhalation. Allow it to spread to every cell of your body, soothing and cleansing as it goes. Focus on the area of your heart, and allow the white light to soothe and calm your heart chakra. Continue meditating until you feel that all the stress and tension in your body has been released.

The Trinity Chakras

The top three chakras of the trinity vibrate at a higher level than the four chakras of the quatern. They relate to the three quadruplicities of astrology, known as cardinal, fixed, and mutable. The cardinal signs are Aries, Cancer, Libra, and Capricorn. They are all outgoing and energetic. The fixed signs are Taurus, Leo, Scorpio, and Aquarius. They are determined, patient, loyal, and reliable. The mutable signs are Gemini, Virgo, Sagittarius, and Pisces. They are adaptable, resourceful, and communicative.

Highly evolved people make use of all seven chakras. However, most people are unwilling to invest the necessary time and energy to develop their brow and crown chakras, and work mainly with the lower five chakras.

Throat Chakra (Visshudha)

Color: Blue
Element: Sound
Quadruplicity: Fixed
Functions: Communication, creativity
Glands: Thyroid and parathyroid
Petals: Sixteen
Sense: Sound
Desire: Inner peace
Gemstone: Turquoise
Challenge: To risk
Keyword: Concepts

The throat chakra is located at the level of the throat. The Sanskrit word Visshudha means "pure." The throat chakra relates to communication and self-expression, especially when spoken. It constantly searches for the truth in all things.

When the throat chakra is well balanced, the person will feel contented and be kind and considerate to others. When the throat chakra is overstimulated, the person will be overbearing, sarcastic, and arrogant. When the throat chakra is understimulated, the person will be weak, uncommunicative, devious, and unreliable.

When the throat chakra is not functioning as it should be, the person may suffer from sore throats and colds or have problems with the sinuses, thyroid, or ears.

The throat chakra is stimulated whenever you use your voice. Consequently, singing, talking, shouting, and screaming are all effective ways to energize and recharge this chakra.

You will need a piece of moonstone to calm your throat chakra. Sit in a straight-backed chair with your feet flat on the floor and your knees creating approximately a ninety-degree angle. Use both hands to hold the moonstone against your throat. Close your eyes and visualize the unwanted energy being released from your throat chakra and absorbed by the moonstone. Visualize this for at least two minutes, and repeat daily for as long as necessary.

Brow Chakra (Ajna)

Color: Indigo
Element: Light
Quadruplicity: Mutable
Functions: Intuition, thought, perception
Gland: Pituitary
Petals: Ninety-six
Desire: To be in harmony with the universe
Gemstones: Lapis lazuli, quartz
Challenge: To turns one's dreams into reality
Keyword: Intuition

The brow chakra is located in the forehead, just above the eyebrows. The Sanskrit word Ajna means "command."

The brow chakra governs the mind and looks after the other chakras. This chakra is frequently called the "third eye," as it is concerned with psychic and spiritual matters. We can pick up other people's thoughts, feelings, and intuitions with the brow chakra.

When the brow chakra is overstimulated, the person is proud, authoritative, and dogmatic. When it is understimulated, the person is timid, hesitant, and unassertive.

When the brow chakra is not functioning as it should be, the person may suffer from headaches or have problems with his or her vision.

The brow chakra can be stimulated with a piece of amethyst. Sit in a straight-backed chair with your feet flat on the floor and your knees creating approximately a ninety-degree angle. Place the amethyst in the area of your third eye, close your eyes, and visualize energy passing from the amethyst into your brow chakra. Slowly move the amethyst in small circles in a clockwise direction for about sixty seconds.

To calm and soothe your brow chakra, lie on your back, close your eyes, and take slow deep breaths until your body feels totally relaxed. If necessary, visualize all stress and worry leaving your body with each exhalation.

Crown Chakra (Sahasrara)
Color: Violet
Element: Thought
Quadruplicity: Cardinal

Function: Union with the Divine
Gland: Pineal
Petals: Nine hundred and seventy-two
Desire: Universal understanding
Gemstones: Amethyst, diamond
Challenge: To grow in knowledge and wisdom
Keyword: Spirituality

The crown chakra is located at the top of the head and is often depicted as a halo when artists paint someone who is spiritually evolved. The Sanskrit word Sahasrara means "thousand." The symbol of this chakra is the thousand-petaled lotus.

The crown chakra harmonizes and balances the often conflicting sides of our nature. It also helps us gain insight into the interconnectedness of all living things. The crown chakra remains dormant until all the other chakras have been mastered and are in a state of balance. When the crown chakra is balanced, the person experiences enlightenment and gains a sense of being at one with the universe.

When the crown chakra is overstimulated, the person will feel frustrated and depressed. When this chakra is understimulated, the person will be withdrawn and find it hard to experience any joy in life.

When the crown chakra is not functioning as it should be, the person may suffer from apathy, listlessness, or depression.

To stimulate the crown chakra, lie on your back with your eyes closed. Starting with the root chakra, visualize each of your chakras in turn. See them all perfectly balanced, and notice the colors of each one. After visualizing the brow chakra, take a deep breath, hold it for as long as you can, and say "Om" as you slowly exhale.

To calm and soothe the crown chakra, sit in a straight-backed chair with your feet flat on the floor and your knees creating approximately a ninety-degree angle. Cup a piece of rose quartz in your hands and close your eyes. Focus on your breathing for sixty seconds, and then shift your attention to the rose quartz in your hands. Visualize a gentle, relaxing, and cooling energy coming from the crystal and moving into every cell of your body. Conclude the exercise by raising your hands and holding the crystal to the top of your head for a few seconds. Take three slow, deep breaths and open your eyes.

Meditation, prayer, and periods of quietness all help you gain a closer connection with your crown chakra and become aware of your divine nature.

There are seven rays and seven main chakras. We'll look more at the magical and mystical number seven in the next chapter.

CHAPTER FIVE

THE POWER OF SEVEN

THE NUMBER SEVEN HAS appeared many times in this book already. We've discussed the seven main colors of the aura, the seven main chakras, and the seven rays. It would seem that this number is important and significant.

Seven has been considered a sacred and mystical number since well before recorded history. According to the Bible, the creation of the world took seven days. The ancient Babylonians and Egyptians gazed in awe at the seven sacred planets they could see in the sky. The ancient Egyptians also venerated seven Wise Ones. These were seven hawks who flew upwards from the eye of Ra, and looked after knowledge and learning.[1]

The word seven is derived from the Greek word *sebo,* which means "to venerate." The Hebrew word *shaba,* "to swear," comes from the same root as the number seven and can be interpreted as "to come under the influence of seven things."[2] This shows that the number seven was considered so powerful that oaths were made using it. The ancient Greek historian Herodotus wrote that the Arabs made their oaths over seven stones that had been smeared with blood.[3] Another example of this can be found in the first book of the Bible when Abraham and Abimelech met at Beersheba to swear an oath. "And Abraham set seven ewe lambs of the flock by themselves" (Genesis 21:28).

In the second century BCE, the Greek poet Antipater of Sidon listed the Seven Wonders of the World: the Great Pyramid of Giza, the Hanging Gardens of Babylon, the Statue of Zeus at Olympia, the Colossus of Rhodes, the Temple of Artemis at Ephesus, the Mausoleum at Halicarnassus, and the Lighthouse of Alexandria. It's highly likely that he chose seven wonders, rather than six, or eight, or twelve, because of the symbolic qualities of the number seven.

There were also Seven Wise Men of Greece. These were seven sages who lived between 620 and 550 BCE. They were Bias, Chilon, Cleobulus, Periander, Pittacus, Solon, and Thales. However, even when Plato created this list, there was much disagreement about who should be included. Yet again it seems that seven were chosen because of the symbolism of the number.

Seven in Christianity

The number seven appears frequently in the Bible. There were the seven days of Creation. "An on the seventh day God ended his work which he had made; and he rested on the seventh day from all his work which he had made. And God blessed the seventh day, and sanctified it: because that in it he had rested from all his work which God created and made" (Genesis 2:2–3). God told Cain that if anyone killed him, "vengeance shall be taken on him sevenfold" (Genesis 4:15). Pharaoh dreamed about seven plentiful years followed by seven years of famine in Genesis 41.

Seven played an important role in the fall of the walls of Jericho. God said to Joshua: "Seven priests shall bear before the ark seven trumpets of rams' horns: and the seventh day ye shall compass the city seven times, and the priests shall blow with the trumpets. And it shall come to pass, that when they make a long blast with the ram's horn, and when ye hear the sound of the trumpet, all the people shall shout with a great shout; and the wall of the city shall fall down flat" (Joshua 6:4–5).

The first deacons of the early Christian church were "seven men of honest report, full of the Holy Ghost and wisdom" (Acts 6:3).

Jesus turned seven loaves of bread and a few small fish into a feast that fed four thousand people. The meat that was left over filled seven baskets (Matthew 15:34–38).

When Peter asked Jesus if he should forgive his brother seven times, "Jesus saith unto him, I say not unto thee,

Until seven times: but, Until seventy times seven" (Matthew 18:22).

There are also several references to seven in the Book of Revelation, the final book of the Bible. These include the seven churches of Asia (1:11), seven golden candlesticks (1:12), seven stars (1:16), seven lamps of fire (4:5), seven Spirits of God (4:5), seven seals (5:1), a lamb with seven horns and seven eyes (5:6), seven angels with seven trumpets (8:2), seven thunders (10:3), a red dragon with seven heads and seven crowns (12:3), seven plagues (15:6), seven golden vials (15:7), and seven kings (17:10). There are also seven petitions in the Lord's Prayer (Matthew 6:9–13).

Christian interest in the number seven explains the seven joys of the Virgin Mary, the seven sorrows of the Virgin Mary, the seven spiritual works of mercy, and the seven words from the cross.[4] The seven deadly sins—lust, gluttony, greed, sloth, wrath, envy, and pride—were also part of the teachings of the early Church. Pope Gregory is one of many teachers who used this list of sins to help people lead godly lives.

The number seven appears in early Christian literature, too. A fifth-century legend called *The Seven Sleepers of Ephesus* was extremely popular during the Middle Ages, as it affirmed the Christian belief in the resurrection of the dead. In this story, seven Christian soldiers were sealed inside a cave during the persecution of Christians in the time of Emperor Decius (about 250 CE). The soldiers fell into a miraculous sleep that lasted more than 150 years. When the cave was opened during the reign of Theodosius II (408–450 CE), the soldiers woke up. After explaining to the emperor the Christian interpretation of their experience, they died. The emperor was impressed and pardoned all the bishops who had been persecuted for believing in the Resurrection.

In medieval times there were also Seven Champions of Christendom. These were the national saints of seven countries: St. George (England), St. Andrew (Scotland), St. Patrick (Ireland), St. David (Wales), St. Denys (France), St. James, the son of Zebedee (Spain), and St. Anthony of Padua (Italy).

The Most Famous History of the Seven Champions of Christendom by Richard Johnson (1598) was one of the most popular books of its time. It contained heavily embellished stories of the lives and achievements of the seven saints. The number seven features frequently in the book, too. St. George was imprisoned for seven years, and St. Denys lived inside a hart for seven years. St. James was dumb for seven years. St. Anthony was freed of his enchantment when the seven lamps were dowsed using water from an enchanted fountain. St. Andrew rescued six women who had spent seven years as white swans, and St. David slept for seven years in an enchanted garden.

Seven in Islam

The Kabah is a square-shaped building in the center of the great mosque in Mecca. During the Hajj, an annual pilgrimage to Mecca that all devout Muslims intend to make at least once in their lifetime, pilgrims walk around the Kabah seven times in a counterclockwise direction.

In addition to this, pilgrims walk between Mount Safa and Mount Marwah seven times. This is to commemorate Hagar, the mother of Ishmael, who ran between these two hills looking for water to help save the life of her son. Fortunately, an angel arrived, and a well appeared where the angel touched the ground. The water it produced saved both mother and child.

Pilgrims also visit Mina, which is just outside Mecca. Here they throw seven pebbles at each of the three walls that represent the Devil.

In Islam there are seven skies, seven seas, and seven layers of the earth. There are also seven heavens. They are:

1. **Pure silver.** This is the home of Adam and Eve.

2. **Pure gold.** John the Baptist and Jesus are here.

3. **Pearl.** Joseph lives here. Azrael, the Islamic angel of death, also lives here.

4. **White gold.** Enoch, who became Metatron, the king of angels in Christian belief, is called Idris in Islam. He rules the fourth heaven. The Islamic Angel of Tears lives here, too.

5. **Silver.** Aaron, the brother of Moses, rules the fifth heaven. The Islamic Avenging Angel lives here, too.

6. **Ruby and garnet.** This heaven is ruled by Moses. The Guardian Angel of Heaven and Earth lives here. This angel is composed of both snow and fire.

7. **Divine light.** The seventh heaven is ruled by Abraham. Every inhabitant of this heaven has 70,000 heads. Each head has 70,000 faces, each face has 70,000 mouths, each mouth 70,000 tongues, and each tongue can speak 70,000 languages, all of which continually chant the praises of Allah.

There are seven levels of hell and seven doors leading to hell.

There are seven major sins in Islam. These come from a *hadith,* or report, from the Prophet Muhammad. They are polytheism (worship of many gods), witchcraft, killing a soul that Allah has forbidden to be killed, riba (usury), unlawfully taking the money of an orphan, running away from the field of battle, and slandering chaste, innocent women.

Seven in the Bahá'í Faith

Bahá'u'lláh (1817–1892), the founder of the Bahá'í religion, wrote a book called *The Seven Valleys,* which describes the seven mystical stages a follower must go through to find God. The seven valleys are:

1. The Valley of Search

2. The Valley of Love

3. The Valley of Knowledge

4. The Valley of Unity

5. The Valley of Contentment

6. The Valley of Wonderment

7. The Valley of True Poverty and Absolute Nothingness

Seven in Judaism

The *Sepher Yetzirah,* also known as the *Book of Creation* or the *Book of Formation,* is the oldest book of Jewish esotericism. It was probably written between 200 and 500 CE, although Jewish tradition says it was written by Abraham. This book confirms the Jewish belief that seven is an extremely powerful number: "God has loved and blessed the number seven more than anything beneath heaven."[5] The *Sepher Yetzirah* says that God created the seven days of the week, the seven orifices of perception, seven heavens, and seven planets.[6]

The Hebrew word for luck is *gad.* This is equal to the number seven in gematria, a form of numerology in which letters have numerical values. Interestingly, *mazel,* the other Hebrew word for luck, equals 77.[7]

Seven appears in Jewish weddings, too, since there are seven wedding blessings and seven circuits of the groom. There are also seven days of festive meals after the wedding. When someone dies, there are seven days of mourning.

The menorah is the most ancient symbol of Judaism, as God revealed it to Moses. It is a seven-stemmed candleholder, and its shape represents the burning bush (Exodus 3:2–4).

The Talmud contains the Seven Laws of Noah, also known as the Noachide Laws, which are intended for all humankind. According to Jewish belief, any non-Jew who follows these laws will be considered a Righteous Gentile and be guaranteed a place in the world to come. These laws are:

1. Thou shalt not commit idolatry.

2. Thou shalt not blaspheme God's name.

3. Thou shalt not commit bloodshed.

4. Thou shalt not steal.

5. Thou shalt not commit incest or adultery.

6. Thou shalt establish courts of justice.

7. Thou shalt not eat the flesh cut from a living animal.

Seven in Hinduism

In the Hindu tradition, the world mountain has seven faces, and the sun has seven rays. The seventh ray symbolizes the power of God. Surya, the sun god, rides a chariot pulled by seven horses, each symbolizing a color, an energy, and a day of the week.

In Hinduism there are seven truths, which include living peacefully, freedom of thought, respect for nature, respect for all animals, becoming one with Brahman, and the belief that our good and bad actions will ultimately affect us.

There are seven vows or promises in a Hindu wedding. There are also seven holy cities, seven sacred places, seven sacred rivers, and seven famous battlefields.

There are fourteen worlds, or planes of existence. The Earth is the lowest of the seven higher worlds, and beneath it are seven lower worlds (underworlds or hells). When someone dies, the god of death measures the person's good and bad deeds and determines which heaven or hell the soul should go to. The god of death also determines how long the soul has to remain there before being reborn.

The seven higher worlds relate to the chakras and the seven layers of the aura.

Earth is the eighth world and is inhabited by living human beings. It relates to Muladhara (root chakra).

Bhuvarloka, the middle world of air, is the ninth world. It is inhabited by celestial beings. It relates to Svadisthana (sacral chakra).

Suvah, or heavenly world of the sky, is the tenth world. It is inhabited by devas (gods). It relates to Manipura (solar plexus chakra).

Maharloka, or world of radiant beings, is the eleventh world. It relates to Anahatha (heart chakra).

Janaloka, or world of deities, is the twelfth world. It relates to Visshudha (throat chakra).

Tapoloka, or world of pure souls, is the thirteenth world. It relates to Ajna (brow chakra).

Satyaloka, or world of truth, is the fourteenth world. It relates to Sahasrara (crown chakra).

The seven lower worlds (hells) are Atala, Vitala, Sutala, Mahatala, Tatatala, Rasatala, and Patala.

Seven in Buddhism

According to legend, Buddha took seven steps when he was born. In 477 BCE, when Buddha felt that his Nirvana was close, he went to the town of Kusinara and stood on a stone facing south. His feet left an impression on the stone. Copies of his footprints can be found in temples throughout India, China, and Japan. Seven auspicious signs were observed in his footprints, and these are called the Seven Appearances. They are the conch shell, the crown of Brahma, the diamond mace, a fish, a flower vase, a swastika, and the Wheel of the Law.

Seven in Japanese Lore

The Japanese have Seven Gods of Good Luck who bring happiness as well as good fortune. Six of the gods are men, and Benten, the goddess of music, is a woman. They are often depicted traveling on a treasure ship known as Takarabune. The Seven Gods of Good Luck give gifts to honest, worthy people every New Year.

Seven in China

The seventh month of the lunar year is known as the Ghost Month. At this time of year, the ghosts of the dead are able to return and mingle with the living. During this month, people burn paper offerings to the dead. These can depict anything; examples include paper money, paper houses, paper cars, or paper television sets. On the fifteenth day of the month, huge food festivals are held to please and placate the hungry ghosts. Any concerts held at this time contain empty seats for the ghosts to sit in. Any music played at this time is loud, as ghosts appreciate this. By the end of the month, it is hoped that all the ghosts will have returned to the underworld.

In China, young women look forward to the Feast of the Double Seventh, which occurs each year on the seventh day of the seventh lunar month. An ancient tradition says that magpies gather to form a bridge across the Milky Way, so the Weaving Maiden can visit her lover, the Cowherd. The Weaving Maiden is the patroness of unmarried women, and on this day young girls bring her various gifts and have their fortunes told, hoping that this will be the last time they have to do it. The Weaving Maiden and the Cowherd are popular subjects for Chinese artists.

There are many versions of the story of the Weaving Maiden and the Cowherd. One tells of how a young cowherd came across seven girls bathing in a pool. He took the clothing of one of the girls and hid where he could watch them. When the girls finished their swim, they clothed themselves in feathers and flew up into the sky. The one girl without clothes remained behind, and Niulang, the cowherd, discovered she was Zhinu, the seventh daughter of the Goddess of Heaven. The seven sisters had come down to earth in search of fun, as life in heaven was rather boring. Niulang and Zhinu fell in love, married, and had a son.

When the Goddess of Heaven discovered that her seventh daughter had married a mere mortal, she was furious and ordered her to return to heaven. The cowherd was devastated, until one of his cows told him to kill her and use the cow's hide to fly after her. The cowherd did this, and he and his son were reunited with Zhinu in the sky. They were so happy together that Zhinu completely forgot to carry out her daily task of weaving beautiful clouds. The Goddess of Heaven angrily scratched a line through the heavens to separate Niulang and Zhinu. This created the Milky Way. The Goddess decided they should see each other only once a month. She asked a magpie to deliver this message. Unfortunately, the magpie forgot it was once a month and told them they could meet only once a year.

Ever since then, the lovers have met on the evening of the seventh day of the seventh month in the lunar calendar. Magpies gather to create a bridge across the Milky Way. In China, this has become the annual feast day of young girls, one of the biggest events in the Chinese year.

In China, the number seven also plays an important role after someone dies. It takes up to 7 x 7 days for the person's soul to finally leave the body, as it needs to break its connection with the world and the person's family before it can move on. Every seventh day, up to and including the forty-ninth day, sacrifices and rituals are held to ensure that the soul leaves the body and makes its way into the next world.

Seven in Folklore

The Irish hero Cúchulainn had seven fingers on each hand, seven toes on each foot, and seven pupils in each eye. He was seven years old when he was given his first weapons, and his son, Connla, was seven years old when his father killed him.

According to British folklore, the Queen of the Fairies pays a tithe to Hell every seven years. Thomas the Rhymer lived in the world of the faeries for seven years.

The seventh son of a seventh son is traditionally believed to possess special powers. In Ireland, he had the gift of healing. In the United Kingdom, he possessed magical powers and a gift for divination. In Central America, it was believed he would become a werewolf.

Children's fairy tales often use the number seven as well. "Snow White and the Seven Dwarfs," "The Seven Ravens," and "Seven at One Blow" are good examples.

The Seven Wise Masters is a collection of Oriental stories dating from the tenth century. In this book, Prince Lucien returns home after receiving instruction in the seven liberal arts by seven wise masters. His astrological forecast told him that he could die if he spoke in the next seven days. One of the women of the court tried to seduce him, but was turned down. She lied to the king about this, and the prince was condemned to death. The wise masters managed to have the sentence suspended by one day. However, the spurned woman further embroidered her story, and the one-day suspension was disallowed. The wise masters appealed again and again until the seventh day, and Prince Lucien was able to tell the true story of the attempted seduction. The prince was acquitted, and the woman who had attempted to seduce him was condemned to death instead.

One of the most famous examples of the number seven in folklore appears in this traditional children's nursery rhyme:

As I was going to St. Ives
I met a man with seven wives.
Each wife had seven sacks,
Each sack had seven cats,
Each cat had seven kits:
Kits, cats, sacks, wives—
How many were going to St. Ives?

Seven as Superstition

Many craps players refuse to say the word seven while gambling, as they believe it will bring them bad luck. Instead of saying "seven," they refer to it as "the Devil" or "it."

A common superstition says that breaking a mirror will bring seven years of bad luck. This superstition dates back to Roman times. They believed that the mirror reflected the person's soul. If the mirror broke, the person's soul would be trapped inside the remains of the mirror.

The Seven Senses

"It is enough to fright you out of your seven senses."
—*François Rabelais*

"You frighten me out of my seven senses."
—*Jonathan Swift*

"Huzzaed out of my seven senses."
—*Joseph Addison*

"I am almost frightened out of my seven senses."
—*Miguel Cervantes*

The concept of seven senses dates back to the Stoics' philosophy of the soul. The Stoic school of philosophy was established in Athens in 308 BCE. The Stoics believed the soul comprised seven parts, which were housed in different parts of the body. Both Philo of Alexandria (c. 20 BCE–c. 50 CE), the Jewish theologian and philosopher, and Claudius Galen (c. 130–c. 201 CE), the Greek physician, referred to the seven parts of the soul.[8]

An ancient tradition says that the soul, or the "inward holy body," comprises seven properties, which are directed and influenced by the seven visible planets.[9] The properties are:

1. **Fire.** This animates (body movement, sense of balance).

2. **Earth.** This provides feeling.

3. **Water.** This provides speech.

4. **Air.** This provides taste.

5. **Mist.** This provides vision.

6. **Flowers.** These provide hearing.

7. **South Wind.** This provides the sense of smell.

Consequently, the seven senses are animation, feeling, speech, taste, vision, hearing, and smell. These are described in the Apocrypha as: "They received the use of the five operations of the Lord [sight, hearing, taste, smell, and feeling], and in the sixth place he imparted them understanding, and in the seventh speech, an interpreter of the cogitations thereof" (Ecclesiasticus 17:5).[10]

Seven in Numerology

Pythagoras is generally considered to be the father of numerology. He considered seven to be "the vehicle of life," as it consists of a triangle (three) and a square (four). Three and four are also considered auspicious numbers in numerology, and symbolize body and soul, spirit and matter.[11] Seven is also indivisible, which means it's not directly related to any other number between one and ten.

Over time, seven came to symbolize perfection, completeness, and spirituality. It is also the number of introspection, insight, analysis, understanding, and wisdom. In numerology, every number possesses both positive and negative qualities. The negative side of the number seven is aloofness, a critical approach, inability to express one's feelings, lack of trust, uneasiness in social situations, and a strong desire to work on one's own, with little or no input from others.

In the next chapter, we'll combine everything we've learned so far, and start working with the soul.

CHAPTER SIX

WORKING WITH YOUR SOUL

NOW IT'S TIME TO put everything we've discussed together. The first step is to look at the seven rays and determine which ray or rays you resonate to. Here is a questionnaire that will help you discover which rays you are using most in this lifetime. Answer each question with a 0 to 5. A 5 means your answer is a strong "yes," while a 0 means the question is not relevant for you in this lifetime.

Here are the questions:

1. Do you like to be in charge? 0 1 ②3 4 5

2. Are you tactful and diplomatic? 0 1 2 3 4 ⑤

3. Do you enjoy discussing your ideas with others?
   0 1 2 3 4 ⑤

4. Do you find it easy to help others resolve their differences? 0 (1) 2 3 4 5

5. Are you a clear, logical thinker? 0 1 2 3 (4) 5

6. Are you loyal? 0 1 2 (3) 4 5

7. Do you work best in a tidy, well-organized environment? 0 1 2 3 (4) 5

8. Are you a leader? 0 1 2 (3) 4 5

9. Are you sympathetic and compassionate? 0 1 2 3 (4) 5

10. Are you broad-minded? 0 1 2 3 4 (5)

11. Do you have a good imagination? 0 1 2 3 4 (5)

12. Did you enjoy mathematics at school? (0) 1 2 3 4 5

13. Are you an optimist? 0 1 2 (3) 4 5

14. Do you enjoy complicated, detailed work? 0 1 2 3 (4) 5

15. Are you an independent thinker? 0 1 2 3 4 (5)

16. Are you tolerant of others? 0 1 (2) 3 4 5

17. Are you good at dealing with money? 0 1 2 3 4 (5)

18. Do you have an aesthetic sense and appreciate beauty? 0 1 2 3 4 (5)

19. Do you enjoy researching and analyzing? 0 1 2 3 4 (5)

20. When you make up your mind to do something, do you persist until you have achieved it? 0 1 2 3 (4) 5

21. Do you enjoy ritual and ceremony? 0 (1) 2 3 4 5

22. Do you have a strong sense of where you're going in your life? 0 1 2 (3) 4 5

23. Do you love humanity as a whole? 0 1 (2) 3 4 5

24. Do you enjoy analyzing problems and creating effective solutions? 0 1 2 3 4 (5)

25. Are you growing spiritually as you progress through life? 0 1 2 3 4 (5)

26. Are you a logical thinker who can put all emotions to one side while working on a problem? 0 1 (2) 3 4 5

27. Are you an idealist? 0 1 2 3 (4) 5

28. Are you able to manifest your desires? 0 1 2 3 4 (5)

29. Are you courageous? 0 1 2 (3) 4 5

30. Are you able to remain serene and worry-free when problems are occurring in your life? (0) 1 2 3 4 5

31. Are you constantly full of ideas? 0 1 2 3 4 (5)

32. Are you able to captivate others? 0 1 2 3 (4) 5

33. Are you as good with your hands as you are with your mind? (0) 1 2 3 4 5

34. Are you able to focus on a task and carry it all the way through to completion? 0 1 2 3 4 (5)

35. Do you see yourself as powerful? 0 1 2 3 4 (5)

36. Do you stand up for what you believe in? 0 1 2 3 4 (5)

37. Are you good at teaching others the skills that you possess? 0 1 2 3 (4) 5

38. Are you, or would you make, a good businessperson? 0 1 2 3 (4) 5

39. Can you express yourself well with words on paper? 0 1 2 3 4 (5)

40. Do you have many technical skills? 0 1 2 ③ 4 5

41. Do you have a strong faith? ⓪ 1 2 3 4 5

42. Are you patient, and prepared to wait until the time
is right before taking action? 0 1 2 ③ 4 5

Once you've completed the questionnaire, you can find
out which ray or rays you are on.

2 3 5 3 3⁵ Questions 1, 8, 15, 22, 29, and 36 relate to the first ray. *2 1*

5 4 2 2 0₄ Questions 2, 9, 16, 23, 30, and 37 relate to the second *1 7*
ray.

5 55 55⁴ Questions 3, 10, 17, 24, 31, and 38 relate to the third *29*
ray.

1 55 5 4⁵ Questions 4, 11, 18, 25, 32, and 39 relate to the fourth *25*
ray.

4 05 20³ Questions 5, 12, 19, 26, 33, and 40 relate to the fifth ray. *14*

3 3 4 45⁰ Questions 6, 13, 20, 27, 34, and 41 relate to the sixth *19*
ray.

4 41 55³ Questions 7, 14, 21, 28, 35, and 42 relate to the seventh *2 1*
ray.

You may find that one ray is much stronger than the
others. This means you are primarily on this ray.

You may find that two or three rays are all stronger than
the others. This shows that you are learning the lessons of
these rays in this lifetime.

It's possible for all the rays to be approximately equal in
strength. This is unusual, but it can happen. If this occurs,
read the descriptions of the seven rays in chapter 3 to see if

you can determine which is the strongest and consequently your primary ray.

Other Ways to Determine Your Ray

There are several other ways to determine your personal soul ray(s).

Occupation

Your choice of occupation can frequently give you a clue as to your personal ray. This is especially the case if you've always been attracted to a certain type of career. This applies even if you are not currently engaged in that particular career. The armed forces, for instance, are listed under the first ray. If you always wanted to be in the army, navy, or air force, but circumstances prevented you from following this career, it may still indicate that you are a first ray person.

First Ray

Armed forces

Police

Security

Politics

Leader

Entrepreneur

Second Ray

Teacher

Healing professions

Mentor
Philanthropist
Researcher

Third Ray
Philosopher
Economist
Businessperson
Judge
Scholar
Astrologer
Organizer
Banker

Fourth Ray
Mediator
Psychologist
Artist
Musician
Writer
Architect

Fifth Ray
Scientist
Lawyer
Engineer
Inventor
Researcher
Mathematician

Sixth Ray

Evangelist

Missionary

Mystic

Orator

Zealot

Seventh Ray

Administrator

Builder

Producer

Politician

Designer

Magician

Priest

Problem Solving

People on different rays resolve their problems in specific ways.

First Ray

Force

Willpower

Giving orders

Overpowering opposition

Making decisions with little input from others

Second Ray

Negotiation

Intuition

Gentle persuasion
Nonresistance
Creating empathy

Third Ray
Logic
Creating a plan of action
Lengthy thought and analysis
Adaptability
Strategy
Ability with words

Fourth Ray
Charm
Captivating others
Dramatizing the situation
Creating an illusion of vulnerability
Creating harmony
Reconciling the situation

Fifth Ray
Research
Scientific approach
Observation and analysis
Patient review of the facts
Experimentation
Slow, deliberate thought

Sixth Ray
Single-mindedness
Spiritual guidance
Ability to inspire and persuade others
Sacrificial approach

Seventh Ray
Finely tuned, deliberate approach
Good organization
Highly detailed approach
Ability to create order
Magic

Negative Qualities

Everyone possesses a mixture of positive and negative qualities. People who are not living up to their full potential frequently exhibit more of their negative, rather than their positive, potential. Many people fail to recognize their negative traits. If this applies to you, then you may need to ask a friend to help you determine your negative qualities. If you feel you can do this on your own, your negative traits will provide information as to the particular ray or rays you happen to be on in this lifetime.

First Ray
Arrogance
Pride
Impatience
Selfishness

Egotism

Extravagance

Rigidity and obstinacy

Stubbornness

Domination

Second Ray

Impracticality

Unassertiveness

Overprotectiveness

Fearfulness

Inferiority complex

Sentimentality

Self-pity

Self-sacrificing

Third Ray

Indecision

Aloofness

Cunning

Deceit

Cruelty

Opportunism

Overly critical

Carelessness

Dishonesty

Fourth Ray

Lack of confidence

Excessive worry

Rapidly changing moods
Self-indulgence
Impracticality
Moral cowardice
Lack of motivation
Frequent inner conflict

Fifth Ray
Self-centeredness
Critical
Pedantic
Materialism
Coldness
Skepticism
Prejudice
Uneasy in social situation

Sixth Ray
Impulsiveness
Intolerance
Fanaticism
Overly dependent
Overly idealistic
Inability to adapt
Gullibility
Low self-esteem

Seventh Ray
Materialism
Regimentation

Extravagance
Pomposity
Need to conform
Intolerance
Perfectionism

Purpose of the Soul

The soul is guided by the interests and qualities of the particular ray, or rays, it is using in this lifetime. Each soul is different, of course, but here are the main desires and potentials of souls that work with specific rays. If your soul is working on two or more rays, then you'll have to read the potentials of each one.

First Ray Soul Purpose

The purpose of first ray souls is to provide leadership, motivation, and strength to others. These souls work for the benefit of humanity as a whole. They are benevolent, generous, steadfast, and firm when necessary. These souls have enormous vision and are usually concerned with the overall picture rather than the details. Consequently, they sometimes appear detached and unconcerned about problems that other souls consider important. They enjoy freedom and hate being constricted or limited in any way. They have a strong connection with the Divine and constantly strive to uphold spiritual ideals and principles. Their greatest desire is to carry out divine will in this incarnation. Although the latent talents of first ray souls are obvious to everyone who knows them, few of them achieve anywhere near their full potential.

Second Ray Soul Purpose

The purpose of second ray souls is to serve, counsel, teach, and advise others. These souls possess a deep love of humankind and work hard to help others grow and achieve their full potential. These souls are selfless and tend to put other souls first. As second ray souls work best when helping others, they are frequently found in people who work in humanitarian-type careers. They almost always work best in a partnership, and seek the love, comfort, and security of marriage and friendship, as this gives them security as well as a good base to work from. Second ray souls instinctively sense that all humanity is connected, and we should all love one another. They also have a powerful love for the Divine and enjoy a strong connection with the source of all life.

Third Ray Soul Purpose

The purpose of third ray souls is to encourage the creativity and intellect of others. They enjoy helping people raise their sights and realize what they are truly capable of. These souls gain enormous satisfaction from creating and participating in actions that are in keeping with the divine plan. Third ray souls solve their problems using reason, logic, and analysis. Despite working according to a plan, third ray souls are flexible and adaptable and fit in easily with others. Their greatest satisfaction frequently comes from the sheer joy of thinking about a problem and coming up with a good, practical solution. Despite this strong love of logic, third ray souls still have a strong sense of the sacred and desire a closer connection with the Divine.

Fourth Ray Soul Purpose

The purpose of fourth ray souls is to create harmony and unity in the world. These souls enjoy bringing peace and happiness into the lives of others. They are selfless, loving, altruistic, compassionate, and tolerant. They find it easy to fit in and relate well with others, as they take people as they find them. They are able to see both sides of a situation and can empathize with everyone concerned. All souls can speak through the person's conscience, but fourth ray souls seem to do this more effectively than souls on other rays. Fourth ray souls have a strong sense of beauty and try to create it in everything they do. They possess a strong sense of the sacred and see the presence of the Divine in everything that is beautiful, peaceful, and meaningful.

Fifth Ray Soul Purpose

The purpose of fifth ray souls is to make good use of innovation and technology to improve the lives of all humanity. They can lose themselves in scientific and technical research, as they have total faith in their ability to use their inventions and discoveries for the benefit of others. They are happiest when they make a new discovery or experience a revelation as a result of their intellect. They enjoy problems, because they see them as challenges that can be resolved scientifically. They also gain enormous pleasure as a result of successfully solving them. They are fascinated with the mysteries of the world, and hope to be involved in deciphering them. They constantly see the Divine in the wondrous and beautiful natural world. These souls live by the concept that "the world is my church, and life is my prayer."

Sixth Ray Soul Purpose

The purpose of the sixth ray soul is to selflessly inspire and motivate others to live up to their greatest potential. These souls are idealistic and altruistic and possess a great love for humanity. Because they are so idealistic, they refuse to accept anything less than perfection. Sixth ray souls are enthusiastic and encouraging and derive great satisfaction from the success of others. They express their love freely and are devoted to the recipients of their love and friendship. Even if they don't receive love and friendship in return, they still place the objects of their devotion on a figurative pedestal, where they can admire and love them.

Seventh Ray Soul Purpose

The purpose of the seventh ray soul is to help others organize and manage their own lives more effectively. This helps them gain vision and clarity, and they become much more successful as a result. Seventh ray souls are selfless. They invariably play an important role inside groups, teams, and organizations, where their selflessness enables them to work for the benefit of everyone in the group. They respect and value others and treat them with courtesy, friendship, and love. Seventh ray souls gently direct others to become aware of their spiritual nature and to always do what is right. Seventh ray souls enjoy establishing and maintaining system and order, as they are naturally tidy and well organized.

How to Experience the Rays

The following meditations will help you become attuned to the energies of the different rays. Start with the ray that resonates most with you before experimenting with the others.

Relaxation Exercise

You need to be in a quiet, meditative state before you can experience the energies of the different rays. Set aside at least thirty minutes of time during which you will not be disturbed. Make sure the room you are in is pleasantly warm, and wear comfortable, loose-fitting clothes. Make yourself as comfortable as possible. You might like to do this progressive relaxation exercise in a recliner chair, or perhaps lying on the floor. I find it difficult to perform these exercises while lying in or on a bed, as I tend to fall asleep. Consequently, although you need to be warm and comfortable, you don't want to be so relaxed that you drift off to sleep. Temporarily disconnect the phone to avoid being disturbed during the exercise.

Take three slow, deep breaths, holding each breath for a few seconds before exhaling. Close your eyes and allow your body to relax. Become aware of your breathing, and notice how each breath helps you to relax. Focus on your eyes, and allow the fine muscles around your eyes to relax.

Once you have done this, focus on your left foot, and allow the toes on this foot to relax. You may feel a tingling sensation in your toes as you do this. Once your toes are relaxed, allow the pleasant feeling of relaxation to gradually spread throughout your foot, until your entire left foot is relaxed.

Repeat this with your right foot, until both feet are completely relaxed. Focus on your left foot again, and allow the feeling of relaxation to drift upwards, over your ankle and into your calf muscles. Allow the relaxation to drift over your knee and into your thigh. Once you feel your entire left leg is totally relaxed, repeat the process with your right leg.

Both of your legs should now be completely relaxed. Allow the relaxation to drift into your abdomen, your chest, and into your shoulders.

Focus your attention on your left arm, and allow the relaxation to drift down your arm and into your hand and fingers. Repeat with the right arm.

Allow the relaxation to drift into your neck, your face, and all the way up to the top of your head. Focus on your eyes again, and let them relax as much as you possibly can.

Finally, mentally scan your entire body to make sure that every part is completely relaxed. If you find any areas of tension, gently focus your attention on the tension until it dissolves.

You are now completely relaxed, and every muscle in your body is loose and limp. Everyone is different. Some people find it easy to relax, while others need more time. It's not a race, and it doesn't matter how long it takes to relax your body. Although I can now become completely relaxed in a matter of seconds, I usually prefer to take several minutes to complete the process, as I enjoy the sensation of relaxation slowly drifting through my body.

If you haven't performed a progressive relaxation exercise before, you might want to practice this a few times before moving on to the next stage of experiencing the energies of each ray. If you want to finish at this point, for any reason, all you need do is tell yourself that you're returning to your everyday life on the count of five. Slowly count from one to five, open your eyes, and allow yourself to become familiar with your environment again. When you feel ready, get up and carry on with your day. Have something to eat and drink before returning to your everyday tasks. I have a glass of water and a few raw almonds. Although you can return to conscious awareness by simply counting from one to five, you might want to add a few words as well, perhaps along these lines:

"One. Gaining energy and feeling fine. Two. Feeling good about every aspect of my life. Three. Becoming familiar with my surroundings. Four. Almost back. And five. Eyes opening and feeling great."

If you are continuing with the exercise, here are the scripts for exploring the seven rays.

Experiencing the First Ray

"In this nice, calm, peaceful, relaxed state, I can achieve anything I set my mind to, and in this session I'm going to become closer to my soul. I'm going to become aware of my own spiritual energies by experiencing the energies of the seven rays that emanate from the Divine [use whatever word feels right for you, such as God, the universal life force, the Ultimate, Creator, Mother, Father, and so on].

"In this meditation I'm going to feel the energies of the first ray, the Ray of Power and Will. I'll start by experiencing the power and incredible energy of my own personal life force. [Pause, and visualize or imagine your own personal life force. Become aware of it in every cell of your body.] I feel this life force reaching out and connecting with the Divine, enabling me to gain insights into my true purpose in this lifetime. I sense myself moving steadily forward. I'm doing it with greater and greater confidence now as my focus becomes clearer.

"I sense myself working for the greater good of all humankind, working in accord with my divine purpose to further my evolution and growth.

"I feel myself developing the necessary confidence to inspire, motivate, lead, and direct others, to help them find their own path to the Divine. I sense the strength and courage I have deep within to do what is right, to seek what is worthwhile, and to uphold what is true and good.

"I see myself coming up with good ideas, experimenting with new and different concepts, and being prepared to start something new. I feel strong, bold, and unafraid. I feel independent and ready for anything.

"I'm aware of a sense of unbelievable strength that helps me to achieve everything I want to accomplish in this lifetime. I experience physical strength [pause for a couple seconds], mental strength [pause for a couple seconds], and spiritual strength [pause for a couple seconds].

"I have unlimited energy and am aiming higher now, higher than ever before. I will achieve my goals, and the results will be positive for everyone concerned.

"I feel restored, revitalized, and motivated as a result of spending time with the first ray. I'm excited that I can bask in the energies of the first ray whenever I wish. [Pause for as long as you wish.]

"And now it's time to return to my everyday life. I'll open my eyes on the count of five, feeling stimulated and energized. One. Gaining energy and feeling fine. Two. Becoming aware of my surroundings. Three. Gradually returning. Four. Feeling ready for anything. And five. Eyes opening and feeling wonderful."

Experiencing the Second Ray

"In this nice, calm, peaceful, relaxed state, I can achieve anything I set my mind to, and in this session I'm going to become closer to my soul. I'm going to become aware of my own spiritual energies by experiencing the energies of the seven rays that emanate from the Divine [use whatever word feels right for you, such as God, the universal life force, the Ultimate, Creator, Mother, Father, and so on].

"In this meditation I'm going to experience the energies of the second ray, the Ray of Love-Wisdom. I allow myself to become totally surrounded with loving energy from the universe. I feel every cell of my body becoming filled with pure, divine love. And in this nice, peaceful, relaxed state, I consciously let go of all negativity and allow myself to relax completely in this ocean of love.

"I see myself becoming energized. My love for the universe is apparent in everything I do. I'm ready and willing to help others who need love and a helping hand. My love spreads further and further every day as I give and receive radiant love. I am sensitive and compassionate. I can now understand and feel the joy and suffering of others.

"As I'm surrounded with love, I look at life in a different way now. I'm gaining knowledge and wisdom. I understand at a deeper level than ever before. This understanding enables me to see the essentials of any situation. I can hone in on problems and resolve them using the unlimited energies of understanding, wisdom, and love.

"My intuition is growing and expanding. I can sense the immortal soul in everyone I meet, and I love each and every soul.

"I'm developing patience and moving forward in a steady, gradual, easy fashion. Nothing bothers or disturbs me, as I am calm and serene in every type of situation.

"I feel happy and contented with my progress as a result of spending time with the second ray. I know that I'm developing in exactly the way I should be. It's comforting to know I can bask in the energies of the second ray whenever I wish. [Pause for as long as you wish.]

"And now it's time to return to my everyday life. I'll open my eyes on the count of five, feeling stimulated and energized. One. Gaining energy and feeling fine. Two. Becoming aware of my surroundings. Three. Gradually returning. Four. Feeling ready for anything. And five. Eyes opening and feeling wonderful."

Experiencing the Third Ray

"In this nice, calm, peaceful, relaxed state, I can achieve anything I set my mind to, and in this session I'm going to become closer to my soul. I'm going to become aware of my own spiritual energies by experiencing the energies of the seven rays that emanate from the Divine [use whatever word feels right for you, such as God, the universal life force, the Ultimate, Creator, Mother, Father, and so on].

"In this meditation I'm going to experience the energies of the third ray, the Ray of Active Intelligence. I focus on my powerful mind, and everything it does for me. I appreciate my ability to reason and assess, to focus on problems and resolve them analytically, to think thoughts, both great and small, and to create in my mind anything and everything I desire.

"I see myself communicating with others, expressing myself well, grateful for my ability to express my thoughts in conversation as well as in words on paper. I picture myself using my mind and ability to communicate with others in all sorts of situations, such as making plans, expressing my views, directing others, and helping worthwhile causes.

"I visualize myself thinking and acting quickly, even when under pressure. I can handle complex situations and problems effectively because I detach myself from all emotion and work logically and rationally. I enjoy being busy, and my mind can work on several matters simultaneously. I want to know exactly what's going on, in any situation I find myself in.

"I change quickly when situations and circumstances change. I'm adaptable, flexible, and quick to act.

"I handle money well and enjoy being generous with what I have. I have the ability to make more money than I need, as I enjoy helping others who are less fortunate than I am.

"I am economical and try to achieve as much as possible, with as little as possible. I enjoy achieving good results efficiently and economically.

"I am satisfied with my progress as a result of spending time with the third ray. I know I'm learning, growing, and developing in exactly the way I should be. It's comforting to know I can enjoy spending time basking in the energies of the third ray whenever I wish. [Pause for as long as you wish.]

"And now it's time to return to my everyday life. I'll open my eyes on the count of five, feeling stimulated and energized. One. Gaining energy and feeling fine. Two. Becoming aware of my surroundings. Three. Gradually returning. Four. Feeling ready for anything. And five. Eyes opening and feeling wonderful."

Experiencing the Fourth Ray

"In this nice, calm, peaceful, relaxed state, I can achieve anything I set my mind to, and in this session I'm going to become closer to my soul. I'm going to become aware of my own spiritual energies by experiencing the energies of the seven rays that emanate from the Divine [use whatever word feels right for you, such as God, the universal life force, the Ultimate, Creator, Mother, Father, and so on].

"In this meditation I'm going to experience the energies of the fourth ray, the Ray of Harmony, Beauty, and Art. I realize everyone on this planet experiences conflict from time to time. Even though I know and experience this, I remain focused on harmony and unity.

"No matter what situation I find myself in, I continue to grow and develop spiritually. I learn through struggles, crises, setbacks, and occasional disappointments. I experience personal growth in my body, mind, and soul every time these occur.

"I have the ability to create harmony where there was discord before. I can resolve long-standing difficulties and can reconcile people who are unable to reach an agreement on their own.

"I can see both sides of every situation and have the ability to mediate and facilitate resolutions where there was previously conflict and disharmony.

"I keep my feet firmly on the ground and utilize a practical approach that creates harmony and beauty everywhere I go.

"I have a strong aesthetic sense and enjoy living and working in attractive surroundings. I have a good imagination and use it to create beauty in my environment.

"I gain pleasure and satisfaction from using my creative abilities. I have a strong sense of color and harmony, which could be harnessed into art or music, if I wish. I enjoy writing, and this gives my imagination plenty of room to create good ideas and record them on paper.

"I am naturally intuitive and rely on my hunches and feelings to resolve difficulties and achieve my goals.

"I enjoy entertaining and amusing others with my sense of humor and my unique approach to life. I am spontaneous and sometimes surprise people with what I say and do.

"My greatest pleasure comes from creating peace and harmony in the world I live in.

"I am satisfied with my progress as a result of spending time with the fourth ray. I know I'm learning to handle conflict, so I can reconcile and balance not only my life but also the lives of others. I gain strength and satisfaction whenever I spend time inside the energies of the fourth ray. [Pause for as long as you wish.]

"And now it's time to return to my everyday life. I'll open my eyes on the count of five, feeling stimulated and energized. One. Gaining energy and feeling fine. Two. Becoming aware of my surroundings. Three. Gradually returning. Four. Feeling ready for anything. And five. Eyes opening and feeling wonderful."

Experiencing the Fifth Ray

"In this nice, calm, peaceful, relaxed state, I can achieve anything I set my mind to, and in this session I'm going to become closer to my soul. I'm going to become aware of my own spiritual energies by experiencing the energies of the seven rays that emanate from the Divine [use whatever word feels right for you, such as God, the universal life force, the Ultimate, Creator, Mother, Father, and so on].

"In this meditation I'm going to experience the energies of the fifth ray, the Ray of Concrete Knowledge and Science. This gives me the ability to look at situations in a logical and rational manner. I can analyze, dissect, and think deeply, to gain knowledge and wisdom. I can focus on a problem and resolve it using clarity, insight, and practical common sense.

"My mind is so strong and powerful that I can think of something and immediately create an effective plan to turn it into a reality. I enjoy the accuracy and detail that are necessary to make this happen.

"I enjoy getting below the surface of things to work out the true situation that is hidden beneath. I take little at face value, preferring to make up my own mind after analyzing the situation thoroughly.

"I am detached when necessary. I can think calmly and rationally, without involving my emotions in the process.

"I am inquisitive and have a strong sense of curiosity. I enjoy finding answers by asking questions and investigating. I enjoy research and am persistent and rigorous until I find the answers I'm seeking. I take little on trust, preferring to verify the truth in my own time and in my own way.

"I enjoy technology and love keeping up with all the latest advances in the fields I enjoy. I am practical and prefer a hands-on approach.

"I enjoy explaining what I've learned to others, and gain satisfaction when they understand my ideas, take them on board, and start working with them.

"I am satisfied with my progress as a result of spending time with the fifth ray. I know my rigorous scientific approach enhances not only my life but also the lives of others. I gain confirmation and satisfaction whenever I spend time inside the energies of the fifth ray. [Pause for as long as you wish.]

"And now it's time to return to my everyday life. I'll open my eyes on the count of five, feeling stimulated and energized. One. Gaining energy and feeling fine. Two. Becoming aware of my surroundings. Three. Gradually returning. Four. Feeling ready for anything. And five. Eyes opening and feeling wonderful."

Experiencing the Sixth Ray

"In this nice, calm, peaceful, relaxed state, I can achieve anything I set my mind to, and in this session I'm going to become closer to my soul. I'm going to become aware of my own spiritual energies by experiencing the energies of the seven rays that emanate from the Divine [use whatever word feels right for you, such as God, the universal life force, the Ultimate, Creator, Mother, Father, and so on].

"In this meditation I'm going to experience the energies of the sixth ray, the Ray of Devotion and Idealism. I have the ability to transcend my everyday world and spend time communing with the Divine. My devotion has no bounds. Although I'm frequently let down and hurt, my idealism, faith, and optimism keep me moving forward.

"I have a strong vision of what the world should be like, and I focus on the possibilities and potentials rather than the limitations.

"I focus clearly on what I desire and pursue my goals with persistence and determination. Nothing can distract me once I've made up my mind to do something.

"I am loyal to others, and once I've made a friend, this loyalty becomes an integral part of the relationship. I am sincere, honest, and open with my friends. They know they can rely on me whenever necessary, and I value their belief in my willingness to help.

"I have good self-esteem but remain humble, as I have the ability to see myself exactly as I am.

"I have the ability to inspire and motivate others. I am a natural enthusiast and have the ability to sell my ideas to others. I have the potential to be a powerful force for good, especially in spiritual matters.

"I constantly endeavor to develop spiritually and to gain a closer connection with the Divine. When it comes to important matters, I seek divine help and guidance. This plays an increasingly important role in my life.

"In all ways I try to be good, honorable, kind, devoted, and loving.

"I am satisfied with my progress as a result of spending time with the sixth ray. My idealistic approach and love for all humanity enhance not only my life but also the lives of others. I gain spiritual comfort whenever I spend time inside the energies of the sixth ray. [Pause for as long as you wish.]

"And now it's time to return to my everyday life. I'll open my eyes on the count of five, feeling stimulated and energized. One. Gaining energy and feeling fine. Two. Becoming aware of my surroundings. Three. Gradually returning. Four. Feeling ready for anything. And five. Eyes opening and feeling wonderful."

Experiencing the Seventh Ray

"In this nice, calm, peaceful, relaxed state, I can achieve anything I set my mind to, and in this session I'm going to become closer to my soul. I'm going to become aware of my own spiritual energies by experiencing the energies of the seven rays that emanate from the Divine [use whatever word feels right for you, such as God, the universal life force, the Ultimate, Creator, Mother, Father, and so on].

"In this meditation I'm going to experience the energies of the seventh ray, the Ray of Order and Ceremonial Magic. I know I have the ability to create and maintain system and order. I sense a divine plan that is perfect in every way, and although this is far beyond the ability of humankind to see, let alone understand, I feel a faint glimmering of its system and order.

"I have the potential to achieve anything I set my mind to in this incarnation. With the help of the Divine, I can manifest anything I desire, and I'm prepared to do whatever it takes to achieve it. I desire success on a large scale.

"I enjoy structured activities, regular routines, and rituals that help me achieve my goals. I work well with groups of like-minded people, and enjoy rituals and ceremonies that bring us closer together.

"I am a good organizer. I can communicate my ideas to others, handle the details, manage, delegate, and motivate. I am patient and realize that some things need time to incubate before they can be manifested.

"I am growing and developing as a result of spending time with the seventh ray. My personal power and ability to make good use of system and order enhance not only my life but also the lives of others. I gain strength and power whenever I spend time inside the energies of the seventh ray. [Pause for as long as you wish.]

"And now it's time to return to my everyday life. I'll open my eyes on the count of five, feeling stimulated and energized. One. Gaining energy and feeling fine. Two. Becoming aware of my surroundings. Three. Gradually returning. Four. Feeling ready for anything. And five. Eyes opening and feeling wonderful."

You might feel that friends or acquaintances are experiencing more interesting or important rays than you. This is not the case, as no ray is better than any other, and all seven rays are equally important. The particular ray you happen to be on indicates the lessons and experiences you need to learn in this lifetime.

In the next chapter we'll see how the seven rays work with each chakra.

CHAPTER SEVEN

LAYERS OF THE SOUL

THE RAYS ENTER THE physical body and have an energizing, life-giving effect on every cell. They also have a profound effect on the layers of the aura (the subtle body), especially the chakras. Each ray influences and affects each chakra. In effect, each ray splits into seven parts, one part for each chakra. These can be considered layers of the soul.

The chakras are the energy centers inside the subtle body that receive the energies of the universal life force from the particular ray and then distribute these energies around the body.

No one knows how the universal life force enters the body. As a teenager, I was taught that it entered the body through the crown chakra (at the top of the head) and filtered down to the other chakras through the nadi system that connects them. However, there are other possibilities. In her book *The Complete Book of Chakra Healing*, Cyndi Dale suggests that each ray enters the body in a particular place. The first ray enters through the coccyx, for instance, and the second ray enters through the third eye/forehead.[1] Other people suggest that the rays enter the body through the chakra that relates best to each ray. If this is the case, then the rays enter the body through these chakras:

First ray: Crown chakra

Second ray: Heart chakra

Third ray: Throat chakra

Fourth ray: Root chakra

Fifth ray: Brow chakra

Sixth ray: Solar plexus chakra

Seventh ray: Sacral chakra

How the First Ray Stimulates the Seven Chakras

The first ray is the Ray of Power and Will. It relates strongly to the crown chakra. The positive qualities of this ray are courage, strength, honesty, and leadership.

The root chakra is concerned with survival and the will to live. This includes eating the right foods, exercising, sleeping, and even earning money. The root chakra grounds, or "roots," us to the earth. It provides feelings of security and comfort. The positive qualities of the first ray help the root chakra perform its functions, as they help it feel safe and secure.

The sacral chakra is concerned with creativity, sexuality, and emotional balance. The positive qualities of the first ray enhance the sacral chakra's potential in all of these areas.

The solar plexus chakra is concerned with will, power, and strength. These are all qualities shared with the first ray, which is able to add extra power if and when required.

The heart chakra is concerned with compassion, love, and relationships. The first ray adds steadfastness, honesty, and open-mindedness to enhance the positive qualities provided by a balanced heart chakra.

The throat chakra is concerned with communication, self-expression, and creativity. The first ray enables the throat chakra to speak the truth in a confident, fearless manner.

The brow chakra is concerned with the mind as well as intuitive and spiritual matters. The first ray enables the brow chakra to develop intuitive and spiritual insights and look toward the future with confidence.

The crown chakra is concerned with our spirituality and connection with the Divine. The courage, honesty, and strength of the first ray harmonizes well with the purity of the crown chakra, and helps it to grow in knowledge, wisdom, and understanding of the interconnectedness of all life.

How the Second Ray Stimulates the Seven Chakras

The second ray is the Ray of Love-Wisdom. It relates strongly to the heart chakra. The positive qualities of this ray are calmness, patience, endurance, serenity, intuition, and a love of the truth.

The root chakra is concerned with grounding, solidity, and survival. All the positive qualities of the second ray have a positive effect on the root chakra, enabling it to perform its functions with serenity, calmness, and patience.

The sacral chakra is concerned with pleasure, emotional balance, and sexuality. The second ray aids this chakra by providing patience, when necessary, as well as calmness and serenity.

The solar plexus chakra is concerned with will, power, and strength. The second ray can soften any potential aggressiveness and domination by providing calmness, cooperation, and a sympathetic approach.

The heart chakra is concerned with compassion, balance, love, and relationships. The wisdom and love of the second ray harmonizes perfectly with the energies of the heart chakra.

The throat chakra is concerned with communication, self-expression, and creativity. The insight, wisdom, sympathy, and universal love provided by the second ray are all expressed effectively when combined with the throat chakra.

The brow chakra is concerned with intuition, clairvoyance, and the powers of the mind. The second ray is concerned with intuition, too, and also adds qualities of philanthropy, sympathy, understanding, and universal love.

The crown chakra is our connection to the Divine. This harmonizes perfectly with the second ray qualities of humanitarianism, philanthropy, intuition, wisdom, and spirituality.

How the Third Ray Stimulates the Seven Chakras

The third ray is the Ray of Active Intelligence. It relates strongly to the throat chakra. The positive qualities of this ray are a powerful and creative mind, the ability to see the overall picture as well as the details, good communication skills, adaptability, and financial and business acumen.

The root chakra is concerned with grounding, solidity, and survival. All the positive qualities of the third ray have a powerful effect on the root chakra, enabling it to keep the person grounded while at the same time seeing greater opportunities that can be achieved with the unlimited potential of the mind.

The sacral chakra is concerned with pleasure, emotional balance, and sexuality. The third ray aids this chakra by providing adaptability, creativity, and good communication skills. These all help the sacral chakra to realize its potential, too.

The solar plexus chakra is concerned with will, power, and strength. The third ray aids this chakra by adding the qualities of adaptability, abstract thinking, and a powerful mind. These both soften and strengthen the direct approach of this chakra.

The heart chakra is involved with compassion, balance, love, and relationships. These qualities are considerably enhanced by the good mind and excellent communication skills provided by the third ray.

The throat chakra is concerned with communication, self-expression, and creativity. These are all major characteristics of the third ray. All these qualities are all considerably enhanced by this combination.

The brow chakra is concerned with intuition, clairvoyance, and the powers of the mind. These enhance the creative potential of the third ray. The communication skills provided by the third ray enable the person to express his or her intuitive experiences.

The crown chakra is our connection to the Divine. The qualities of the third ray enable the person to enjoy an even closer relationship with the universal life force.

How the Fourth Ray Stimulates the Seven Chakras

The fourth ray is the Ray of Harmony, Beauty, and Art. This ray relates most strongly to the root chakra. The positive qualities of this ray are the ability to reconcile situations and achieve harmony through conflict, artistic and creative potential, and the ability to captivate and entertain others.

The root chakra is concerned with grounding, solidity, and survival. This chakra provides confidence and persistence to people on the fourth ray. This solid foundation also enables them to develop their creativity and people skills.

The sacral chakra is concerned with pleasure, emotional balance, and sexuality. All of these qualities are enhanced by the ability of fourth ray people to harmonize difficult situations and to get on well with others.

The solar plexus chakra is concerned with will, power, and strength. The people skills of the fourth ray enable the solar plexus chakra to express itself more diplomatically and with concern for the well-being of others.

The heart chakra is involved with compassion, balance, love, and relationships. The innate harmony and cooperation provided by the fourth ray enhance all of these qualities.

The throat chakra is concerned with communication, self-expression, and creativity. The people skills, creativity, and aesthetic approach of the fourth ray enhance the communication and self-expression skills of the throat chakra.

The brow chakra is concerned with intuition, clairvoyance, and the powers of the mind. The beauty and harmony expressed by the fourth ray enhance the intuitive qualities of the brow chakra.

The crown chakra is our connection to the Divine. The ability of the fourth ray to grow spiritually through difficulties enhances this connection. The fourth ray's strong aesthetic sense enables the crown chakra to see spirituality in all creation.

How the Fifth Ray
Stimulates the Seven Chakras

The fifth ray is the Ray of Concrete Knowledge and Science. It relates strongly to the brow chakra. The positive qualities of this ray are its common sense, powerful intellect, and ability to objectively analyze, discriminate, and assess information in a clear yet detached manner.

The root chakra is concerned with grounding, solidity, and survival. The practical, objective, and precise qualities of the fifth ray enhance the ability of the root chakra not only to survive but to expand and grow.

The sacral chakra is concerned with pleasure, emotional balance, and sexuality. The analytical approach of the fifth ray enhances the sacral chakra's potential for emotional balance.

The solar plexus chakra is concerned with will, power, and strength. The insight, technical capabilities, and commonsense approach of the fifth ray enhance all of the qualities of the solar plexus chakra.

The heart chakra is involved with compassion, balance, love, and relationships. The scientific, analytical approach of the fifth ray enables the heart chakra to remain balanced while expressing love and compassion.

The throat chakra is concerned with communication, self-expression, and creativity. The powerful, discriminating intellect provided by the fifth ray enhances the potential of the throat chakra for creativity and self-expression.

The brow chakra is concerned with intuition, clairvoyance, and the powers of the mind. The powerful intellect and down-to-earth approach of the fifth ray enable the brow chakra to develop its intuition in a balanced, impartial manner.

The crown chakra is our connection to the Divine. The clear, focused, investigative intellect provided by the fifth ray enhances the crown chakra's connection with the universal life force.

How the Sixth Ray
Stimulates the Seven Chakras

The sixth ray is the Ray of Devotion and Idealism. It relates strongly to the solar plexus chakra. The positive qualities of this ray are humility, sincerity, loyalty, idealism, and a strong faith.

The root chakra is concerned with grounding, solidity, and survival. The solidity and grounding of the root chakra are considerably enhanced by the sincere, loyal, humble, and idealistic qualities of the sixth ray. The strong faith provided by this ray is also enhanced by the solidity and grounding effect of the root chakra.

The sacral chakra is concerned with pleasure, emotional balance, and sexuality. The qualities provided by the sixth ray enhance the emotional balance, pleasure, and sexuality of this chakra.

The solar plexus chakra is concerned with will, power, and strength. The idealism, love, and devotion of the sixth ray balance and harmonize the strength, will, and power of the solar plexus chakra, creating a powerful combination. The unyielding persistence of the sixth ray further strengthens this combination.

The heart chakra is involved with compassion, balance, love, and relationships. The idealism and devotion of the sixth ray harmonize perfectly with the energies of the heart chakra.

The throat chakra is concerned with communication, self-expression, and creativity. The sixth ray energies allow the throat chakra to express itself with humility, idealism, love, and devotion.

The brow chakra is concerned with intuition, clairvoyance, and the powers of the mind. The idealism and love of the sixth ray enable the brow chakra to develop and grow in spirituality and wisdom.

The crown chakra is our connection to the Divine. The humility, idealism, and devotion of the sixth ray enhance and strengthen the connection with the Divine. The persistence of the sixth ray helps in this regard, too.

How the Seventh Ray Stimulates the Seven Chakras

The seventh ray is the Ray of Order and Ceremonial Magic. It relates strongly to the sacral chakra. The main quality of this ray is the energy it has to create order. It can plan, organize, pay attention to details, motivate, and manifest whatever it desires.

The root chakra is concerned with grounding, solidity, and survival. The energy and power of the seventh ray motivate and stimulate the root chakra to help it achieve its goals.

The sacral chakra is concerned with pleasure, emotional balance, and sexuality. This is the chakra that relates to the seventh ray, and it uses the energy this ray provides to organize its activities, scheduling time for pleasure as well as hard work.

The solar plexus chakra is concerned with will, power, and strength. This harmonizes well with the seventh ray's practicality and ability to organize, manage, and achieve its goals.

The heart chakra is involved with compassion, balance, love, and relationships. These qualities help the seventh ray achieve order. The organizational skills provided by the seventh ray help the heart chakra achieve harmony and balance in its relationships.

The throat chakra is concerned with communication, self-expression, and creativity. All of these qualities help the seventh ray to create and maintain system and order. The communication skills of the throat chakra enable the seventh ray to express its needs to coordinate, manage, and motivate others.

The brow chakra is concerned with intuition, clairvoyance, and the powers of the mind. The practicality, power, and reasoning ability of the seventh ray broadens and balances the intuition and psychic potential of the brow chakra. This is a powerful combination, as answers can be provided by both logic and intuition.

The crown chakra is our connection to the Divine. The seventh ray has a close connection with the ultimate life force, too, and this enables the ray to use its soul nature to manifest its goals on the physical plane. This is a form of white, or good, magic. This is why the seventh ray is called the Ray of Order and Ceremonial Magic.

A Day with Your Soul

This exercise will help you learn more about your chakras and your soul. You will also gain a closer connection with the Divine.

You will need to set aside some time on your own for this exercise. A whole day would be ideal, but if you can't spare that amount of time, set aside as much time as possible. You can do a great deal in a single hour if that is all the time you have.

If you're going to spend more than an hour on this exercise, you'll need to prepare some food and drink. Choose good, healthy, nourishing food. Pick at least one thing to eat that you consider expensive or a luxury. This could be considered a treat or an extravagance. This will enable you to nurture your body as part of the exercise. You might also like to pack some small snacks, such as raw, unsalted nuts, raisins, and fruit.

The drinks can be anything except for alcohol and soda. Water is the best choice, but you might like to take tea, coffee, or some other beverage with you.

You will also need pen and paper, or some other method to record your experiences.

You should also set an intention for the day. This can be as brief or as long as you wish. Your intention might be to gain a greater connection with the Divine. You might ask to feel the presence of God in your everyday life. You might ask for some indication that you're moving in the right direction. It's a good idea to think about your intention a few days, or a week, before your special day. Write it down and keep it with you, as you may want to enlarge or amend it as different ideas occur to you.

Decide ahead of time where you're going to spend this pleasant day. There may be a spiritual or holy place nearby. If there is, do some research and learn as much as you can about the place before you visit.

You might choose a place you're familiar with, or deliberately decide to visit someplace you haven't visited before. Choose a pleasant setting where you won't be interrupted. If it's a warm day, you may choose to do this exercise outdoors, possibly by a river or the ocean or maybe out in the country. The idea is to do the exercise in pleasant surroundings, away from your normal, everyday life. If possible, do this well away from other people as well. Of course, this may not be possible. It might be mid-winter, or you may not be able to get away from your home. In this situation, you'll obviously have to do the exercise at home.

If you're doing this exercise outdoors, go for a pleasant walk. Take your time and pause to look at anything that interests you. Look for beauty in everything you see. Watch the flight of a bird, the trunk of a tree, the movements of the clouds. Most of the time we're too busy to notice the beauty that surrounds us.

If you're doing this exercise at home, sit in a comfortable place and look at, or hold, something you find attractive. Look at it from different angles and fondle it, if it's something you can hold. Appreciate the work that has gone into the making of it, and remember how and when you obtained it.

When you feel ready, sit or lie down, close your eyes, and think about the beauty you have just experienced. Hold this thought for as long as possible and then become aware of your physical body. Notice if your thoughts of beauty can be felt in any part of your body. You may notice a sensation in the area of your solar plexus, heart, or throat chakras. You may not become aware of any sensation anywhere in your body, and that is fine, too.

The sensation can appear in unusual places. Not long ago, an acquaintance of mine told me that she had noticed a sensation on the tip of her tongue. Someone else told me he'd experienced tingling fingertips on his right hand.

Again, when you feel ready, open your eyes, and have something to eat or drink. Afterwards, write down your thoughts on what you've done so far. If you experienced a sensation in your body, you should write that down. You should also jot down any thoughts that occurred to you while you were communing with nature.

The next stage is to experience the Divine. Whenever possible I like to do this close to running water, such as a stream or the ocean. There is something about the air close to moving water that seems to make it easier for me to make contact. However, this is not always possible, and if I can't do this close to water, I simply imagine myself lying down beside a bubbling brook or listening to waves rolling in to shore.

Make yourself as comfortable as possible. Close your eyes and relax your body as much as possible. One way of doing this is to focus your attention on the fine muscles around your eyes, and to consciously relax them as much as you can. By the time you've done this, you'll find that the rest of your body has also relaxed.

Another method is to consciously relax all the muscles in your body, starting with the toes of one foot and working your way up to the top of your head, relaxing all the muscles in your body in turn.

Once you feel totally relaxed, mentally scan your body to ensure every muscle is as relaxed as possible. Focus on any areas that are not fully relaxed, and allow them to become loose and limp.

Think about your desire to make contact with the architect of the universe, and then let the thought go. Focus on your breathing, and remain quietly expectant. It's natural for your mind to start thinking about matters that are unrelated to what you're trying to do. Buddhists call this "monkey mind." Whenever you notice that your mind has become sidetracked and is thinking about other things, gently bring it back and focus on your breathing again.

The aim is to enter into the quietness and become one with the Divine. This is exactly what holy people do when they practice contemplative prayer. They are not asking God for anything. Their desire, and goal, is to spend time in God's presence.

You may want to communicate with the Divine. Many people have been taught formal prayers that use stilted, formal language. Naturally, you can speak to God in this way, if that is what you want. For most people, there is a better way. Simply open your heart and say whatever you want. When you've finished, stay in the silence for as long as you can before returning to the present.

You may be fortunate and become one with the Divine the first time you try this exercise. It's more likely that you'll experience the frustrating feeling of getting close but not quite reaching your goal. Even if you don't feel you've become closer to the Divine, you'll have learned more than you might think.

When you feel ready, become aware of your physical body and your chakras. Notice what responses they are giving to your quiet contemplation and meditation.

Once you have done this, take three slow, deep breaths and silently count from one to five. Open your eyes and familiarize yourself with your surroundings again. Lie or sit quietly for a minute or two before getting up. Move around for a few minutes, and eat some nuts, raisins, or fruit and drink some water.

Sit down and draw a picture on your pad. There is no need to think about this. Simply pick up your pen and start drawing. When you've finished the drawing, write down everything you can remember about this experiment. If you recall any of the extraneous thoughts that came into your mind during the meditation, write them down, too.

If it's lunchtime, pause and eat your lunch. Pay particular attention to the beauty all around you as you eat.

Once you've finished writing down your thoughts, or have finished your lunch, enjoy some gentle exercise. If you're outdoors, you might go for a walk. If you're indoors, you may have to run in place, do some stretching exercises, or walk up and down a flight or two of stairs.

The next stage is to visualize your soul ray, or rays, coming from the Divine and going into your body, giving you life. After that, you can visualize the ray exerting its influence on all seven main chakras.

Start by making yourself as comfortable as possible. Relax all the muscles in your body. When you feel totally relaxed, visualize yourself sound asleep in bed. Notice your chest rising and falling rhythmically with your breathing. Also become aware of a ray of pure energy that comes from above and totally surrounds you.

As you look at yourself, see yourself gradually stirring. You may stretch and open your eyes for a few seconds. See yourself lying in bed not fully asleep yet not fully awake.

You can look more closely at the ray now. You see that smaller sub-rays head toward each chakra. As you watch, you sense yourself moving along a sub-ray and into your root chakra. You feel totally at peace and relaxed. It makes perfect sense that you are now inside your own root chakra. From this vantage point you can watch your root chakra performing all its functions, and you can also sense the influence your soul ray has on your root chakra. Watch it energize and breathe new life into your root chakra.

You can stay inside your root chakra for as long as you wish. When you're ready, allow your focus to move inside your sacral chakra. Examine all of the chakras in turn. Alternatively, you might want to do this exercise in seven parts, looking at a different chakra each time.

When you've finished, take three slow, deep breaths, count to five, and open your eyes. As before, relax for a minute or two before getting up. Eat some nuts, raisins, or fruit and drink some water.

Make notes of everything you experienced during this meditation. You have visualized your soul in action, and probably have a great deal to think about.

Allow at least half an hour before performing the final exercise. Sometimes I fill in this time by relaxing and thinking about the previous experiments. Usually, though, I do some stretches and then go for a walk, pausing to appreciate anything interesting or beautiful that I see on the way.

When you feel ready, make yourself comfortable and read your intention out loud. Close your eyes and relax. If you're relaxing in a beautiful setting, visualize it in your mind. If you're doing this exercise at home, imagine a pleasant setting. It may be a place you remember, or you might create a pleasant fantasy scene, if you prefer.

Allow your thoughts to come and go. Instead of accepting any of them, let them go as soon as they become conscious. You may like to watch them float up into the sky or perhaps allow them to dissolve. It makes no difference how you let them go, just as long as you pay no attention to any of them. For all intents and purposes, you are a disinterested bystander who pays no attention to these idle thoughts.

It's hard to give an indication of how much time you should allow for this, as everyone is different. However, after a while you'll notice there are fewer and fewer thoughts to discard, and you've entered into a meditative state. Allow yourself to stay in this state for as long as possible. When you notice that extraneous thoughts are starting to appear again, consciously think of your intention. Repeat it to yourself over and over again, like a mantra.

You might like to say your mantra slightly differently with each repetition. You might sing it, place the emphasis on different words, repeat it slowly or quickly, or even say it falsetto. You'll find that the repetition will help you relax even more than before.

When you feel the time is right, stop repeating the mantra and allow yourself to focus on your soul. Take time to think about how it gives life and energizes every single cell of your body. Think of the countless incarnations it has already experienced before deciding to enter your body. Think about the many incarnations it has yet to experience.

Allow yourself to mentally feel your soul in each of the chakras, and thank it for giving you the spark of life, enabling you to take advantage of all the opportunities this lifetime has to offer.

Finally, simply relax for a few minutes, quietly communing with your soul. When you feel ready, take three slow, deep breaths, count to five, and open your eyes.

Before getting up, think about all the things you've accomplished during this special day. When you get up, have something to eat and drink to ground yourself once again.

Before carrying on with your day, write down any notes you wish to make about your experiences.

CHAPTER EIGHT

CONTEMPLATION AND THE SOUL

THROUGHOUT HISTORY, CONTEMPLATION HAS been used to gain wisdom and a closer connection with the Divine. Contemplation played an important role in the teachings of the Greek philosophers. St. Thomas Aquinas wrote: "It is requisite for the good of the human community that there should be persons who devote themselves to the life of contemplation."[1] Contemplation still plays an important role in the lives of Christian mystics.

Contemplation involves thought, but is not exactly the same as thinking. Dictionaries define it as "thoughtful observation." When you're contemplating, your mind is quiet and relaxed, and you're able to observe, reflect, and consider something while remaining in a meditative state.

You will have experienced this state of quiet contemplation while doing many of the exercises in this book.

Contemplation allows you to access information that you could not gain in any other way. Contemplation enables you to draw on your intuition and emotions, as well as your mind. It can help you discover what your heart and soul are trying to tell you.

You can use contemplation to provide answers to a variety of questions. You can ask comparatively simple questions, such as "What can I do to make today a perfect day?" You can also ask more difficult questions, such as "Should I persevere with my difficult relationship?"

You can also use your quiet time to contemplate spiritual matters. This is an excellent way to study spiritual texts, as it enables you to fully appreciate and understand what the writer had in mind. I find it helpful to contemplate writings on the soul. I find it interesting that only small extracts are required. Sometimes a single sentence is all that is necessary, as you quietly contemplate the words, their meaning, and how they relate to you and your everyday life.

You can enter into a contemplative state in many different ways. In fact, you already reach this state on a regular basis without knowing it. Here are two methods I use when contemplating spiritual matters.

Breath Contemplation

Start by choosing a brief passage that appeals to you. (You'll find some quotes on the soul at the end of this chapter.)

Read the passage and then close your eyes. Take three slow, deep breaths and allow your body to relax. Remain aware of your breathing, and allow each breath to quiet your mind.

Open your eyes and read the passage again. Close your eyes and allow the words you've just read to filter through every part of your body. Become aware of your physical body and notice any effects the words have, especially in your throat and heart. Become aware of any sensations you may experience in your chakras. Think about the words you've just read, and ask: "What do they mean to me?"

If necessary, open your eyes and read the passage again. Close your eyes, still your mind by focusing on your breathing, and ponder the words for as long as you wish. Repeat this stage as many times as you wish.

When you feel you've absorbed everything possible from the words you've read, take three slow, deep breaths and open your eyes. If possible, write down your thoughts and any insights you obtained while you were contemplating.

Mandala Contemplation

You will need a pad of paper and some colored pencils, markers, or crayons for the mandala contemplation. Mandalas are designs that were originally drawn to symbolize the universe. Mandala is a Sanskrit word that means "circle." Consequently, mandalas are usually drawn within the confines of a circle. However, mandalas can be drawn in any shape you wish.

Mandalas work well because they enable you to create pictures that come directly from your soul. With a mandala you're able to convert the words you read into picture form. You'll find this revealing and illuminating.

Before starting the mandala contemplation, draw a circle, or any other shape, on your pad of paper. You'll draw your mandala inside this shape. I usually use an upturned plate as a template for my circle.

Start by choosing a text that appeals to you. Close your eyes and focus on your breathing. Allow your mind and body to become completely relaxed.

Open your eyes and read the text again. Close your eyes, breathe slowly and deeply, and meditate on the words you have just read.

When you feel ready, open your eyes and use your intuition to pick up one of the colored pencils. Use it to start drawing whatever you wish inside your mandala. As it's important to draw spontaneously, let your hand draw whatever it wishes. Observe your hand with mild interest, but pay little attention to what is going on. Your hand will know when it's time to put down one pencil and pick up another. Your hand will also know when you're finished.

Read the words again. Close your eyes and meditate on the words for as long as you wish. Open your eyes and see if your hand has a desire to add anything to your mandala. Allow it to pick up a pencil and draw, if that is what it wants to do. The contemplation is over if your hand has no desire to add anything to the mandala.

You need to repeat this last stage of meditation if your hand picked up a pencil and added anything to your mandala.

You may want to study your mandala right away to see what insights it has given you. I occasionally do this, but usually allow a few hours to pass before examining it.

You'll be surprised at the added insights you'll gain from your mandala. If you do this contemplation on a regular basis, you'll build up a valuable collection of mandalas that will provide insights directly from your soul.

Quotes on the Soul

Here are some insights into the soul provided by famous people throughout history.

"Now I was a child good by nature,
and a good soul fell to my lot.
Nay, rather, being good,
I came into a body undefiled."
—*The Wisdom of Solomon 8:19–20 in the Apocrypha*

"The soul is of heavenly origin,
forced down from its home in the highest,
and, so to speak, buried in earth,
a place quite opposed to its divine nature."
—*Cicero,* On Old Age, *translated by E. S. Shuckburgh*

"A man has a soul, and it passes from life to life,
as a traveller from inn to inn,

till at length it is ended in heaven.
But not till he has attained heaven in his heart
will he attain heaven in reality ...
Love does not die with the body ...
it lives for ever and ever,
through incarnation after incarnation."

—*H. Fielding Hall (1859–1917),* The Soul of a People

"The soul is an emanation of the Divinity,
a part of the soul of the world,
a ray from the source of light.
It comes from without into the human body,
as into a temporary abode, it goes out of it anew;
it wanders in ethereal regions, it returns to visit it;
it passes into other habitations, for the soul is immortal."

—*Ralph Waldo Emerson (1803–1882),* Journals

"Being born twice is no more remarkable
than being born once."
—*Voltaire (1694–1778)*

"Either we have an immortal soul, or we have not. If we
have not, we are beasts; the first and wisest of beasts it may
be; but still beasts. We shall only differ in degree, and not
in kind; just as the elephant differs from the slug. But by
the concession of the materialists, we are not of the same
kind as beasts; and this also we say from our own consciousness. Therefore, methinks, it must be the possession
of a soul within us that makes the difference."

—*Samuel Taylor Coleridge (1772–1834),*
"Materialism" in Table Talk

"I simply believe that some part of the human Self or Soul is not subject to the laws of space and time."
—*Carl Jung (1875–1961)*

"Nowhere can man find a quieter or more untroubled retreat than in his own soul."
—*Marcus Aurelius (121–180),* Meditations

"You don't have a soul. You are a Soul. You have a body."
—*C. S. Lewis (1898–1963),* Mere Christianity

"Just as a mirror, which reflects all things, is set in its own container, so too the rational soul is placed in the fragile container of the body. In this way, the body is governed in its earthly life by the soul, and the soul contemplates heavenly things through faith."
—*Hildegard of Bingen (1098–1179)*
in a letter to the monk Guibert

"One certainly has a soul; but how it came to allow itself to be enclosed in a body is more than I can imagine. I only know if once mine gets out, I'll have a bit of a tussle before I let it get in again to that of any other."
—*Lord Byron (1788–1824)*

CHAPTER NINE

SOUL MATES

NO BOOK ON THE soul would be complete without at least some mention of soul mates. Even people who do not believe in reincarnation use the term *soul mates* to describe the type of relationship between two people who appear to be made for each other.

For people who believe in reincarnation, a soul mate relationship is one between two people who have been together in a number of previous lifetimes. Usually the attraction is instant as soon as these two people meet, and the friendship that ensues seems natural and familiar.

Of course, not every close friendship is necessarily a soul mate one. Recently, someone told me that her marriage had ended after three years.

"I thought he was my soul mate," she told me. "But he couldn't have been, as he's no longer in my life."

In fact, they may well have been soul mates. Soul mate relationships do not necessarily last for a lifetime. Once the two people have learned everything they need to learn from the relationship in this lifetime, there is no need for it to continue. If the relationship continued, the two people involved might miss out on other important lessons they have to experience in this incarnation.

Soul mate relationships can change from one lifetime to the next, too. Someone who was your brother last time around might be your daughter this time. Even though the relationships and gender have changed, the two souls will instantly recognize each other.

Other people have told me how worried they are that their soul mate might be living in another country and they might not have the opportunity to meet in this lifetime. Fortunately, this is not a problem. Soul mates don't meet by accident, and your soul mate will come into your life at the right spiritual time to enable you to have the experiences you both need to make maximum progress in this lifetime.

In fact, there is more than one soul mate waiting for you. Ancient teachings say that groups of cells gathered together while waiting to be transformed into souls. When they were in human form, these souls would instantly recognize each other if and when they happened to meet. All the other cells in the group that you belonged to are your soul mates, and you will notice a strong immediate attraction and recognition whenever you meet them.

Soul mates meet each other when the time is right. It may seem unfair when one person meets his or her soul mate at the age of, say, twenty, while someone else has to wait another forty or fifty years. I was fortunate enough to meet my soul mate at the age of twenty, and we have been married now for more than forty years.

However, an old school friend of mine married twice and had a string of unhappy relationships before finally meeting his soul mate at the age of fifty-eight.

"I envied you," he told me. "I just didn't seem to get it right. However, it finally worked out, and in many ways I'm grateful for all of my previous relationships. I made lots of mistakes, and learned from each one. I can really appreciate my soul mate now. If I'd met her thirty years ago, I'd probably have lost her again because of my immaturity and self-centeredness."

Obviously, the universe waited until my friend was ready before allowing him to meet his soul mate. Consequently, you'll need to remain patient if you're still waiting for your soul mate to appear. You, and your soul mate, may have a number of things that have to be resolved before you can get together. Remember that there are a number of soul mates waiting for you, and when the time is right, you'll finally meet.

Twin Souls

The concept of soul mates dates back thousands of years. In his *Symposium,* Plato wrote that people had been looking for their soul mate ever since Zeus cut them in half. In his mythical story, Plato tells of a world that contained men, women, and people who were both male and female. Plato told how humans began discussing how they could climb up to heaven and replace the gods. Not surprisingly, the gods were upset when they heard this, and discussed what they should do. The simplest solution was to destroy humankind. Fortunately, Zeus came up with a better idea. He suggested cutting all the people in half. This would, he said, immediately double the number of people making offerings to the gods. It would also weaken the people and prevent them from carrying out their plan.

The gods agreed, and all the people were divided into two. Naturally, the people were upset, and Zeus decided to enable each half to enjoy intercourse with their opposite, symbolically creating a whole. As a result, the males sought other males, the females other females, and the people who had been both male and female also sought their other half.

The concept of twin souls dates back to this story. Your twin soul is your other half, dating from when we were all whole. Although the term *twin souls* is mentioned frequently, it is most unlikely that you'll meet your twin soul in this incarnation. This is because your twin soul comes into your life when you are both experiencing your final lifetime on this earth plane.

A twin soul relationship is a perfect one in every way, because you connect on the physical, mental, emotional, spiritual, and soul levels. You can imagine how incredible this must be when you think that most relationships begin when the partners meet on two levels, and in many relationships there is no connection on any level. You will experience this incredible joy one day, but that day may be many incarnations from now. In the meantime, though, you can experience a deeply rewarding, fulfilling, and joyful relationship with one of your soul mates.

William Shakespeare's *Romeo and Juliet* is a good fictional example of a soul mate relationship. However, you don't have to look far to find true examples of soul mate relationships. One of my favorites, as it involves two poets I love, concerns Robert Browning and Elizabeth Barrett Browning.

Robert Browning (1812–1889) was thirty-three years old when he met Elizabeth Barrett (1806–1861). She was six years older than him, and looked much older than her years. At the time they met, she was bedridden and was looked after by her pious father, who said lengthy prayers at her bedside every night and forbade her from ever marrying. Robert and Elizabeth corresponded for four months before she consented to meet him. She was a recluse and was concerned about the effect her appearance would have on him.

The initial meeting went well, and on the following day Robert wrote her a letter saying that he hoped he hadn't offended her or stayed too long. One day later, he wrote her another letter proclaiming his love.

The relationship developed with daily exchanges of letters that gradually became less formal and more intimate. Before long, Robert was writing to "My own, dearest love." After she told him the sad story of her brother's death by drowning, Robert wrote: "Let me say now—this only once—that I loved you from my soul, and gave you my life."[1]

Because her father was adamant that she should never marry, Elizabeth and Robert were forced to elope. After their marriage, they settled in Florence, Italy, and focused on their writing careers. Their son, Robert Barrett Browning, who later became a well-known sculptor, was born in 1849. One year later, Elizabeth's most famous work, *Sonnets from the Portuguese,* was published. This book of sonnets proclaims her love and devotion to her husband. It was written during their two-year courtship, but she did not present it to him until three years after their wedding. Robert's pet name for Elizabeth was "Little Portuguese." This was because she had written a poem called "Catarina to Camoens," which contained the feelings of a dying Portuguese girl for her absent lover.

Sonnets from the Portuguese includes her most famous sonnet, which describes the intense love and devotion she felt for Robert:

> *How do I love thee? Let me count the ways.*
> *I love thee to the depth and breadth and height*

My soul can reach, when feeling out of sight
For the ends of Being and ideal Grace.
I love thee to the level of everyday's
Most quiet need, by sun and candle-light.
I love thee freely, as men strive for Right;
I love thee purely, as they turn from Praise.
I love thee with the passion put to use
In my old griefs, and with my childhood's faith.
I love thee with a love I seemed to lose
With my lost saints,—I love thee with the breath,
Smiles, tears, of all my life!—and, if God choose,
I shall but love thee better after death.

Elizabeth died in 1861, and Robert returned to London, where he continued his career. He died in 1889 and was buried in Westminster Abbey. Two years after his death, two volumes of the letters Robert and Elizabeth wrote to each other were published. They demonstrate conclusively the incredible love they had for each other.

Some writers have asked how an attractive and popular thirty-three-year-old poet, with a wide circle of female friends, could instantly fall in love with a bedridden invalid several years older than himself. Elizabeth delayed the meeting because of concerns about her appearance, but Robert's soul instantly fell in love with her soul, as they had been together in many previous incarnations.

Their love story has been retold many times. The famous play *The Barretts of Wimpole Street* by Rudolf Besier is just one example.

Clara and Robert Schumann are also a good example of a soul mate relationship. Robert Schumann (1810–1856), the famous German composer and pianist, met Clara Wieck (1819–1896), the daughter of his piano teacher, when she was just nine years old. Clara's father disapproved of their friendship and did everything in his power to prevent their relationship from developing. Robert first proposed to Clara when she was fifteen, and three years later, when Clara was eighteen, the couple took Clara's father to court to receive permission to wed. Robert and Clara married in 1840, and Robert Schumann's creativity blossomed as a result. Over the next few years, he composed his best-known works.

However, a shadow was hanging over them. Within a few years of their marriage, Robert started showing signs of mental illness. He was forced to resign his professorship at Leipzig Conservatory. In 1854, he tried to commit suicide by jumping into the Rhine River and was placed in a mental asylum. Clara was forced to go on concert tours to earn enough money to support their family of seven children. Robert wrote to her every day but was not allowed to see her, as it was thought it would make his illness worse. Finally, after almost two and a half years, Clara persuaded his doctors to let her visit. She wrote in her diary: "He smiled at me and put his arm round me with great difficulty, for he had almost lost all control of his limbs. Never shall I forget that moment. I would not give that embrace for all the treasures on earth."[2] Twenty-four hours later, he died.

Robert Schumann had pleaded with her to marry their mutual friend Johannes Brahms, but she refused to do so. She spent the rest of her life composing and teaching.

The story of Robert and Clara is a desperately sad one. They were obviously brought together to enable them to learn some powerful karmic lessons. In the process, they composed some of the most beautiful music that has ever been written.

In many cases, soul mates share the same ray. However, this does not always occur, as soul mates come together for many purposes. Soul mate relationships always provide opportunities for both people to grow and develop. Consequently, someone on the first ray (willpower, forceful, dogmatic) may well be a soul mate of someone on the fourth ray (charm, harmony, reconciliation). In this example, the person on the first ray may need to learn how to sway others without being overly demanding, while the partner might need to learn to stand up for him- or herself. Seemingly unlikely combinations enable both partners to learn valuable lessons.

Because these lessons are sometimes painful, it's important to love and nurture your soul. We'll look at that in the next chapter.

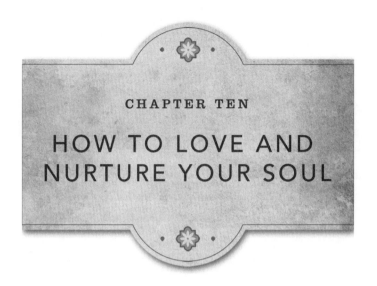

CHAPTER TEN

HOW TO LOVE AND NURTURE YOUR SOUL

CARL JUNG, THE GREAT Swiss psychiatrist, called the soul "the greatest of all cosmic miracles."[1] Yet most people give little if any thought to their immortal souls. The astonishing fact that the soul existed long before the birth of the body, and continues to exist long after the death of the body, is seldom considered. Given this, many people would find it strange to even think about loving and nurturing their soul.

Fortunately, it's not hard to nurture and nourish your soul, and every part of your being will benefit as a result. You'll experience more happiness, joy, and fulfillment in life. You'll gain more pleasure out of everything you do. You'll eliminate stress and negativity and become a more positive, cheerful person. You'll be able to make the most of the present moment, instead of remaining trapped in the past or constantly worrying about the future. You'll also gain a closer connection with the Divine.

I learned the incredible joy of being in the moment from my grandchildren. When they were small, it was impossible to go on a brisk walk with them. They'd stop and gaze, entranced, at the beauty of a spider's web or the flight of a butterfly. They'd watch the movements of a cloud and be absorbed at the different shapes it formed itself into. They'd pick up an acorn or a leaf and enjoy looking at it and handling it. They were, quite naturally, experiencing joy in the present moment.

Every time you allow yourself to experience joy, you're nurturing your soul. There are countless ways of doing this.

Spending time with positive friends who make you laugh nurtures your soul. The laughter provides your physical body with a healthy workout, too. Conversely, spending time gossiping, or discussing grievances with negative people, starves your soul.

Going for a walk, or engaging in any other form of physical activity, is good for your soul. Stay in the moment and try to look at everything as if you were seeing it for the first time. Beauty can be found everywhere, and appreciating and enjoying it does wonders for your soul.

Creating anything is good for your soul, too. Writing and painting are good examples, but what you do doesn't necessarily need to be something that people would term creative. Gardening, cooking, knitting, singing, dancing, playing a musical instrument, humming, journaling, and repairing a broken object are all creative and good for your soul, as long as you enjoy them. I get frustrated doing household repairs, but my son-in-law loves doing them and receives great joy and satisfaction from them. Consequently, he nourishes his soul when engaged in these pursuits, while all I experience is frustration.

Listening to music is a wonderful way to relax and nurture your soul. Reading a good book or watching a good movie also nurtures your soul.

Volunteering your time and/or expertise enables you to help others. Most volunteers report that they get back much more than they give. In addition to the pleasure and satisfaction they receive, their soul benefits, too.

Spending time with the people you love most is one of the best ways to nurture your soul.

You can also nurture your soul by meditating, praying, contemplating, and spending quiet time on your own.

Your soul benefits whenever you do something you enjoy. Consequently, it's impossible to provide a complete list of ways to nurture the soul.

Sometimes people tell me they're too busy to take time out to nurture their soul. I can't imagine why people would choose to starve their soul when all that is necessary is to do something enjoyable.

Here are some specific ways to nurture your soul.

Eye Gazing

If eyes are truly the windows to the soul, it's amazing how few people use them to see the souls of others while at the same time finding a reflection of themselves. Many traditions teach that we are all made in the image of God. Consequently, if you gaze into someone's eyes and see the person's soul, you'll also see God. In the Hindu tradition, eye gazing is called *Darshan,* which means "seeing God, while being seen by God."

Everyone who has been in love has experienced the delight of gazing into the eyes of their partner. By doing this, the two people involved have opened themselves up and revealed their soul to their opposite half. It's a practice that lovers should follow throughout their lives together, but sadly, few people do.

Recently I spoke with a lady who told me about the last few hours of her husband's life. He was dying of cancer and had asked to go home to spend his last days with his loved ones. He could barely speak, and the family made a bed for him in the downstairs living room, as he was incapable of walking up stairs.

At about six in the morning, he called out to his wife in a strong, clear voice. She rushed downstairs, and he greeted her with a big smile on his face. He looked ten years younger than he had the night before. She climbed into bed with him, and for the next three hours they lay together, gazing into each other's eyes. At the end of that time he took a few gasping breaths, and, still gazing into his wife's eyes, he died.

"We gazed into each other's eyes throughout our marriage," she told me. "Whenever times were tough, or one of us needed reassurance or comfort, we'd cuddle and look at each other's soul."

Jalāl ad-Din Muhammad Balkhi (1207–1273), better known as Rumi, is remembered today mainly because of his famous love poems. Rumi was a poet, mystic, theologian, and jurist. He was a keen advocate of eye gazing and wrote: "Whenever two are linked in this way there comes another from the unseen world."[2]

You don't need to be passionately in love to practice eye gazing. All you need is a willing partner who is prepared to experiment with you. Obviously, it needs to be someone who is willing to accept your gaze, and to return it, without feeling awkward or uncomfortable.

Sit facing each other at a distance that feels right for both of you. You might like to start at a distance apart where you cannot quite touch hands. Take a few slow, deep breaths and then gaze at the other person's face. Stay as relaxed as possible, and gradually focus on the other person's eyes. You might like to look at one eye first, and gradually expand your gaze to look into both eyes. You cannot do this for any length of time without absorbing the other person's energy. Your partner will receive your energy in return. Ultimately, you'll become aware of the universal life force, and discover that God, by whichever name you use, is everywhere. This is unlikely to happen the first time you experiment with this, but it will occur when the time is right.

You can also perform eye gazing on your own by sitting in front of a large mirror. You'll find this both healing and restorative. When you do this, gaze at yourself in a loving, compassionate, and gentle way, appreciating yourself for the wonderful creation you are.

Some people have told me they find it hard to gaze into someone's eyes, or even their own eyes, for any length of time. Practice is all that's required to overcome this difficulty.

Some people experience a variety of sensations, even mild pain, in different parts of their bodies. These are the vestigial memories of long-forgotten negative experiences and emotional pain. As you relax and release stress and tension, these sensations will gradually disappear. Because of this, eye gazing can be used to heal yourself, and others, of emotional pain.

Kindness

Most of us give little thought to the needs of the people we encounter as we progress through life. Of course, we pay attention to the needs of friends and loved ones, but we seldom think about the stresses and difficulties other people experience in their lives.

It costs nothing to smile at a stranger. A kind word can make the world of difference to someone who is feeling lonely. The simple act of listening can be a form of kindness.

When we were first married, my wife and I owned a small motel. An elderly lady stayed with us for several months. She was shy, and it took her a while before she'd talk to us freely. Gradually we learned about her sad and lonely life. One day, her nephew arrived and took her home to live with his family. When she left, she thanked us for our kindness. "You're the only people who've ever listened to me," she said. I felt guilty, as sometimes I'd been busy and hadn't wanted to listen to her stories.

An old proverb says you shouldn't criticize others until you've walked a mile in their shoes. You naturally become kinder if you try to imagine what life must be like for the person you are interacting with.

You should also be kind to yourself. Most of us are our own worst enemies, as we constantly sabotage ourselves with negative thoughts.

Your soul benefits from every act of kindness you perform, no matter how small. My boss's secretary, at the first job I had after leaving school, had an office that overlooked a busy street. Several times a day she'd run downstairs and put a coin into a parking meter. When I asked her why she did it, she told me that it made her feel good. She was performing good deeds for people she'd never met and would probably never meet. Putting money in the meter saved these people from receiving a parking ticket, and she hoped they would pass on the favor by doing something to help someone else. It was a good lesson for me, and one I've always remembered.

Another advantage of practicing kindness is that it makes you feel good. That is the whole premise of Charles Dickens's book *A Christmas Carol.* When you feel good, every aspect of your life improves, and you'll start spreading happiness everywhere you go.

The Dalai Lama said: "My religion is very simple. My religion is kindness." Thousands of years ago, Aesop, the Greek writer of fables, wrote: "No act of kindness, however small, is ever wasted."

Make a deliberate effort to be kind for a whole week, and record any changes you experience in your life. At the very least, you'll feel better about yourself, and you'll be more tolerant and understanding of others. If you deliberately practice this for four weeks, you'll find that kindness will become a habit and the benefits will multiply. It would be hard to find a better way to nurture your soul.

Gratitude

Several years ago, I received a letter from a good friend who was dying from cancer. He briefly mentioned the chemotherapy treatment he was undergoing and then told me how grateful he was to have had the gift of life. Because of that, he'd been able to laugh, love, and follow his dreams. He'd built up a good business and married the girl of his dreams, and together they'd had three children. He told me he was sad to be dying decades sooner than he'd expected, but he was full of gratitude for all the gifts and opportunities he'd had. "Life is such a precious gift," he wrote. "I just wish I'd appreciated it more when I was fit and well."

Most of us are too busy with everyday life to pause and think about all the things we should be grateful for. We have the gift of life, for instance. Most of us have family and friends. We possess the necessary skills to earn a living and support our families and lifestyles. We all have skills and talents of various sorts. I have a friend who finds it hard to write a simple sentence but is able to build or repair anything using wood. I admire his practical skills and have called on him many times to fix household problems. In return, I've been able to write letters and reports for him. I'm grateful to have him as a friend.

It is highly beneficial for your soul when you sit down quietly and think about all the things you are grateful for. You'll probably start by thinking about the gifts of life, health, family, and friends. When it comes to people, think about them individually rather than simply expressing thanks for having good friends.

Once you've covered these, you might start expressing gratitude for your job, home, car, hobbies, and the people you work with. However, you can go much further than this. You can think about the person who delivers your daily paper, mows your lawn, and serves you coffee at a local café, and all the other people you interact with. I always include bookstores and libraries, as well as the staff who work at them, when I think about gratitude. After this, I think about the people who write, edit, publish, print, and distribute books.

Can you go even deeper? You can express gratitude for the farmers who provide your food and for the people who built your home, car, and computer. You can think about the people who deliver your mail, collect your garbage, clean the roads and sidewalks, and prepare and serve food at your favorite restaurants. Since my health scare, I include my gratitude for doctors, nurses, and everyone else involved in healthcare. That includes the people who design and develop the latest advances in medicine as well as the hospital orderlies, who also fulfill a vital role.

There is virtually no end to the list of people you could thank for their role in making your world the way it is. When I tried to explain the concept of gratitude to my three-year-old granddaughter, she told me she'd like to thank the person who made the beaches. I agreed with her. We definitely should express our gratitude to the universal life source for providing us with beautiful beaches, mountains, forests, oceans, and everything else that makes this planet such a wonderful place for us to live.

I usually think of all the things I'm grateful for when lying in bed at night. As soon as I start thinking thoughts of gratitude, I feel calm and at peace. I'm sure this helps me enjoy a better night's sleep, since I fall asleep with happy thoughts in my mind.

Generosity

About twenty years ago, I was attending a convention in New Orleans. At the end of the day, four of us walked to a nearby restaurant and enjoyed a good meal. On our way back to our hotel, we were approached by a beggar. Three of us moved away from him, but the fourth stopped and chatted with the man for a couple of minutes. At the end of the conversation, he gave the beggar twenty dollars, and we continued on our way.

One of the others asked him why he'd given the man anything, let alone a significant sum of money. I'll never forget Ken's reply: "Because it made me feel good. I've found that being generous nurtures my soul."

I can't remember much else that happened at that convention, but I'll never forget what Ken did that evening. His actions certainly had an effect on me, and I've been more generous ever since as a result.

Generosity doesn't have to involve money. You can be generous with your time, energy, compassion, and love. When my children were small, one of my son's friends told us that his dad seldom spent time with him, as he was too busy. I thought, at the time, how sad that was. My father was busy, too, but he always made time to watch his children play sports or act in a school play. I sometimes have to make an effort to be generous with my time, but when I do, it always makes me feel good and nurtures my soul.

Be Happy

I was very fortunate to have a wise mentor named Tai L'au. One of his favorite sayings was: "If you want to be happy, be happy." These deceptively simple words are sometimes hard to put into practice. It can be difficult to be happy when everything appears to be going wrong in life, but it can be done. Your soul dislikes negativity and pessimism. It thrives on positivity and joy. Your soul is happy when you're happy. When you're looking ahead with optimism rather than focusing on your problems, your soul feels nourished and fully alive.

Recently I read an article about Dr. Bruce Arroll, a medical professor who was diagnosed with leukemia. He became a patient in a hospital he had regularly visited as a teacher or practitioner. He quickly discovered that "uncertainty is not a good state for the human mind." He decided immediately after the diagnosis that he could choose his attitude. He remained happy throughout the treatment, which was successful. Dr. Arroll said: "I see this as a learning experience. And in some ways I'm grateful to have had it, in a funny sort of way."[3] I'm sure Dr. Arroll's positive attitude and his determination to remain happy no matter what contributed to his full recovery from a life-threatening illness.

I regularly meet people who are going to be happy "one day." They keep postponing happiness until some time in the future, such as when the children leave home or the mortgage is paid off. They're mystified when I tell them they can be happy now if they want to be. It doesn't make sense to postpone happiness. Do yourself, and your soul, a huge favor and resolve to be happy now, no matter what is going on in your life.

Relax

We all know that it's good to relax and unwind, yet few of us consciously relax often enough or even at all. Many people seem to spend most of their lives in a stressed, agitated, and rushed state. If this describes you, you might need to deliberately set aside a few minutes every day in which you simply relax. Let go of all the stresses and worries of your life, and think nothing but pleasant thoughts. You can also relax by doing something you love. My wife relaxes by working in the garden and creating mosaics. I feel totally relaxed when browsing through a used bookstore.

Relaxing restores your body, mind, and soul. I find it much easier to write, for instance, when I'm relaxed, as this allows my thoughts and creativity free play. When I'm stressed out or worried about a particular problem, I find it almost impossible to write. My remedy for this is to go for a walk, listen to some favorite music, or take myself through a relaxation exercise. Once I've taken this time out for myself, I can return to my work and achieve ten times more than I would have if I'd forced myself to continue writing in a stressed state.

Laugh Often

Pablo Neruda (1904–1973), the Chilean poet, wrote: "Laughter is the language of the soul." ("La risa es el lenguaje del alma.") The American poet e. e. cummings (1894–1962) wrote: "The most wasted of all days is one without laughter." Victor Borge (1909–2000), the Danish pianist and humorist, said: "Laughter is the shortest distance between two people."

Laughter is an essential part of life. It's impossible to think about your problems and concerns when you're laughing. It's also highly infectious and brings people together. It relaxes your body, produces endorphins, strengthens your immune system, reduces stress, protects your heart, and nurtures your soul. No wonder people say that "laughter is the best medicine."

Children laugh all the time when they're playing. Adults take life much more seriously. I've even had people tell me they haven't laughed in years.

Fortunately, it's not hard to laugh, if you want to. You can laugh on your own, of course. I laugh out loud when I read something amusing or see something funny on television. When my wife and I travel together, she constantly tells me to keep quiet, as I laugh out loud at comedies I watch on the airplane.

All laughter is good for your soul, but the best laughter occurs when it's shared with others. This is not hard to arrange. All you need do is ask someone if anything funny happened to them recently. Be prepared to reciprocate with a funny story of your own, and you'll both soon be laughing.

Another way to laugh more is to seek out people who laugh frequently. You'll enjoy spending time in their company, and your body and soul will benefit, too.

Laughter is useful in the workplace, too. People who work for someone with a good sense of humor get more work done and suffer less stress than people who work for someone with little or no sense of humor.[4]

Seek out every opportunity you can find to have a good laugh, and your soul will rejoice.

Forgiveness

Everyone has been hurt by others at some time. Sometimes the hurt is deliberate, but it can also be caused unintentionally. Some people are able to forgive and forget easily, but others hang on to the grievance for months, years, or even decades.

I was reminded of this recently when someone sent me an e-mail telling me that a mutual acquaintance had separated from his wife. The e-mail was mischievous, as the person whose marriage had broken up had attacked me on the Internet several years earlier, and the sender thought I'd be pleased to hear the news. Actually, I felt sad, as virtually all marriages begin with love, and it's tragic for both people concerned when those feelings disappear. I was also surprised that it took me several seconds to recall the person he was telling me about. His attacks on me had been hurtful at the time, but I'd forgotten about them years ago.

This was because I'd forgiven him. At the time I was angry and consumed with rage. However, I quickly realized that this created unnecessary stress, made me feel like a victim, and held me back from getting on with my own life. It was a waste of my time and energy. By forgiving him, I didn't condone what he had done. Instead, I released the power this person continued to hold over me as long as I continued to feel resentment and anger. I was slightly surprised that I'd done it so effectively that it took me time to even remember who he was.

Forgiveness may not change the other person, but it will always have a positive effect on you. It will bring peace, serenity, and joy back into your life. Forgiveness is a form of emotional and spiritual healing.

Forgiveness plays a role in every spiritual tradition. The parable of the prodigal son in the Bible (Luke 15:11) is a good example of this. St. Paul wrote about forgiveness in his Epistle to the Colossians: "Forbearing one another, and forgiving one another, if any man have a quarrel against any: even as Christ forgave you, so also do ye" (Colossians 3:13).

A reluctance or inability to forgive has been shown to have a negative effect on a person's health. It creates anxiety, stress, high blood pressure, chronic pain, and depression. It also affects the person's mental health by undermining his or her confidence and self-esteem.

Forgiveness is also good for the soul. Edwin Hubbell Chapin (1814–1880), the American preacher, orator, and author, wrote: "Never does the human soul appear so strong as when it forgoes revenge and dares to forgive an injury."

In the 2009 movie *Invictus,* Morgan Freeman, playing the role of Nelson Mandela, said: "Forgiveness liberates the soul. It removes fear. That is why it is such a powerful weapon." I have no idea if Nelson Mandela ever said this, but he is an outstanding example of someone who practices forgiveness. After twenty-seven years in prison, he was still able to forgive the people who had put him there.

You also should forgive yourself. We've all said and done things that we've regretted later. The feelings of shame and guilt that we impose on ourselves are frequently much greater than the pain we experience when someone hurts us.

If it's possible, make amends. It might be difficult to apologize to someone you've hurt, but it's good for your body, mind, and soul. This is the case even if the other person is unwilling to accept your apology.

By forgiving yourself and others, you'll release all the pain and will be able to move forward in a positive direction and start living again.

Live in the Present

It should be easy to live in the present moment, but most people, myself included, find it hard to do so for any length of time. We're constantly thinking about problems and worries from the past. It's too late now to be concerned about what you should have done or said at some time in the past.

Some people take this to extremes. Some years ago, someone came to me for help, as he was an insomniac. He found
it hard to get to sleep, because the minute he closed his eyes,
he'd think about all the silly things he'd done during the day.
That would remind him of something he'd done a few days
earlier, and that would make him think about how he'd made
a fool of himself the week before. Before long, he was thinking about something he'd done when he was four years old.
No wonder he couldn't get to sleep.

Other people do the opposite, and worry about the
future. How would I manage if I lost my job? What if that
nagging cough is a sign of something serious? Is it safe to
allow my daughter to fly across the country on her own?
These people are concerned about things that will probably
never happen.

It doesn't matter if these people are looking backwards or
forwards. In both cases they're preventing themselves from
living in the present. They're failing to see and appreciate all
the magnificent things that are happening around them at
the present moment.

The remedy is to gently tell yourself that you'll worry
about whatever the concern happens to be at a certain time
in the future. I usually use 7:00 a.m. the following morning.
When the time comes, you'll likely find that the worry has
vanished, as your concern wasn't as important as you thought
it was.

Once you let the concern go, you can live in the present
moment. When you think about it, the present moment is the

only time you ever have. Yesterday is gone, and although the chances are you'll be here tomorrow, there are no certainties.

As you start spending more and more time in the present, you'll find yourself enjoying life much more and will appreciate everything that is going on around you. It's early spring as I'm writing this. Every day I go for a walk. I live right on the edge of a city, which means I can walk in the countryside. It's a wonderful time of year to do this, as I see newborn lambs, baby ducks, courting birds, and spring flowers every day. Because I make a concerted effort to live in the present moment, I'm able to enjoy all of this. If I went for my daily walk full of concerns and worries, I'd hardly notice any of the beauty of the changing seasons around me. I return home revitalized and ready to get back to work.

Living in the present, and making the most of it, nurtures your soul. Someone told me that living in the present makes her soul sing. I like that image, and often think of it, especially when I find myself stressed or worried about something. I tell myself to allow my soul to sing, and deliberately bring myself into the present moment.

CONCLUSION

I HOPE THIS BOOK has helped you strengthen your connection with your immortal soul and enabled you to appreciate everything it has done, and continues to do for you, in this lifetime, as well as the lives you have already lived and the lifetimes you are yet to live. I also hope this book has made you realize that you cannot die. There is life after death. Although I've met many people who say they don't want to come back again, I think most people—believers, agnostics, and atheists alike—secretly hope that death is not the end.

Many near-death experiences occur when the person is clinically dead. The person is no longer breathing and the heart has stopped beating.[1] Consequently, these people have experienced death and returned to life. Apart from anything else, the near-death experience shows that consciousness can exist despite the absence of a functioning brain.

Many near-death experiences begin with the person traveling rapidly through a dark tube or tunnel toward an incredibly brilliant white light. Frequently, the person sees people he or she knew while alive, has a life review, and experiences feelings of love, forgiveness, and acceptance. Usually the person wants to stay inside the light, but somehow the person knows it is not yet his or her time, and returns to earthly life.

So many people have described this scene in books, magazine articles, TV shows, and movies that it cannot be considered a rare experience. More than 2,500 accounts of near-death experiences have been recorded on the Near Death Experience Research Foundation website alone (www.nderf.org).

I was disappointed not to have had a near-death experience. Because my heart had stopped and then started again, I thought I'd come close enough to death to experience one. However, it became clear to me, after discussing this with many people, that although my heart had stopped and started again, I was in the hands of experts who did this sort of thing on a regular basis. Consequently, although my heart stopped briefly, I was in no real danger of dying from that particular procedure. My experience was completely different from that of someone who may, for instance, have died by drowning or in a car accident but was resuscitated by the expertise of modern-day medicine.

Incidentally, I spoke to a number of people who had been returned to life after a major accident or illness and did not remember having a near-death experience. I also spoke to a few people who had left their bodies and were able to look down dispassionately at the people who were trying to save their lives. These people didn't see a brilliant light or experience moving to "the other side."

I was amazed at the number of people I spoke to who've had a near-death experience. I probably shouldn't have been. In 1992, a Gallup Poll found that five percent of the U.S. population have experienced an NDE. This means approximately fifteen million people in the United States have had one.[2]

In every case it was a life-changing experience that, without exception, changed their lives for the better. They lost all fear of death, became more patient, compassionate, and loving, and became more interested in spirituality. They all became convinced that death is not the end, and that there is life after death. Until they had their NDE, many of these people had never before considered the concept of reincarnation.

One of these people, a former criminal, told me that his near-death experience was the best thing that had ever happened to him. It enabled him to see, for the first time, what he was doing to himself and the people who loved him. He now counsels and helps at-risk teenagers.

Another person I spoke to was a multimillionaire. He told me that making money had been an obsession, and it had brought him no happiness whatsoever. "I realized I didn't have a single true friend," he said. "If I'd died on that operating table, no one would have grieved for me." Five years after his operation he is happily married, with an eighteen-month-old son. He looks after his investments and is involved with several charitable organizations.

Many of the people I spoke to had become interested in religion and spirituality as a result of their near-death experience. Some of them had had no interest in religion in the past. However, this experience taught them that death was not the end, and they had a strong desire to learn more about the spiritual side of life. "I don't think anyone would have thought I'd become a believer in reincarnation," one person told me. "Yet it's become one of the most important aspects of my life. I now believe in God, and also believe I'll come back here again and again."

Not surprisingly, a large number of these people became interested in psychic development, and were exploring areas they considered weird or unusual before their experience. "My husband used to have gut feelings," one lady told me. "Only now he calls them flashes of intuition. He's joined a psychic development circle and attends meetings every week. I didn't think anyone as down-to-earth as my John would ever take the psychic world seriously."

Almost everyone I spoke to was experiencing more joy and love in their lives than they had before their near-death experience. "As well as feeling more joy, I've somehow become much more compassionate," one lady told me. "I seem to be able to empathize with other people and their problems now. I never did that before."

Most near-death experiences were fairly similar. Terry, a good friend of mine, told me about what he called his "attempt to get to the other side":

"I was in the hospital for a hernia operation. It was supposed to be a simple procedure, but something went wrong and I almost died. For a brief moment, I felt I was looking down on the operating table. I could see myself asleep with four people bending over me. Almost as soon as I saw that, I found myself in a long tunnel heading toward an incredibly bright light. It was more powerful than anything I'd seen before, but I could look at it without hurting my eyes. I seemed to be moving at breakneck speed, but I still had time to experience feelings of love, compassion, and forgiveness. I felt totally at peace. I knew I was dying or dead, but it didn't matter, as I'd never experienced such bliss before. All I wanted was to reach the light. I felt as if I was returning home. I had no regrets. I was full of joy and reaching out to the light. I was almost there when I heard a strong, deep voice from inside the light telling me it wasn't my time yet. I felt a wave of sadness, and then in the space of a second I was above my body again, and must have returned to it, though I can't remember any more." Terry beamed at me. "You know, when I regained consciousness, I was able to tell the doctors and nurses exactly what they were doing at that moment. The surgeon told me that near-death experiences were common, and he was no longer surprised when a patient mentioned it to him. I know now, without a shadow of a doubt, that there is more to life than we think. I'm a happy man. I have a good life. But I always had a fear of death. That's gone, as I know death is the doorway to a whole new world."

People experience near-death experiences in different ways. Terry didn't mention noises or music. He didn't see any spirits or deceased family members, nor did he experience a review of his life. These are common features in many people's memories.

Terry felt he was inside a tunnel that led to the light. When people who haven't had a near-death experience think about what it must be like, they usually imagine some sort of tunnel. However, a 1982 Gallup poll found that only three percent of people who have had a near-death experience reported being in a tunnel.[3] However, as others reported a swirling sensation or the feeling of being constantly in motion, three percent is probably on the low side.

Constance, a young woman who's studying to become an Episcopalian minister, told me that she did not experience a tunnel. "It was a road, a bumpy road with many twists and turns," she told me. "It was dark, and I was racing along this road. I was knocked and buffeted all the time, but I felt strangely at peace. Ahead, in the distance, I could sense an amazing light, and I knew I was safe and would soon be home." Although Constance did not experience a tunnel, her experience of traveling at great speed along a road in the dark sounds very much like a tunnel.

Many people who have had a near-death experience do not want to come back to their present lifetime. In her book *The Passionate Years,* Caresse Crosby wrote about the time she almost drowned when she was seven years old. As she was drowning, she saw her father and brothers realize what had happened and attempt to rescue her. "I saw the efforts to bring me back to life and I tried not to come back," she wrote. "It was the most perfect state of easeful joy that I ever experienced, then or since … One thing I know, that Nirvana does exist between here and the hereafter—a space of delight, for I have been there."[4]

A day or two after telling me about his near-death experience, Terry phoned to tell me that as a result of the experience he now believed in the soul.

"I never gave the soul a moment's thought before," he said. "It seemed to me we could function pretty well without one. But what was it that traveled into the light if it wasn't my soul? It had to be my soul."

If someone experiences a cardiac arrest, the heart stops circulating blood and the brain ceases to function. At this point, the person's consciousness and ability to reason or remember anything should cease. However, there are now thousands of well-documented exceptions to this.

In 1991, a woman named Pam Reynolds was diagnosed with a life-threatening, inoperable brain aneurysm. Fortunately, Dr. Robert Spetzler, a neurosurgeon in Phoenix, Arizona, offered to help. However, in order to perform the operation, Pam Reynolds needed to be clinically dead for more than an hour. Her body temperature had to be lowered to sixty degrees to stop all vital functions, including brain activity. Pam was clinically dead, as her heart had stopped, she was no longer breathing, and there was no measurable activity occurring in the brain.

Despite all of this, Pam was able to hear the sound of the surgical saw that cut open her skull. She "popped" out of her body while this was going on, and rose over the operating table where she could watch the procedure taking place. She felt she was metaphorically sitting on the surgeon's shoulder as he worked. She could also hear the conversation of the nurses in attendance. At some stage, her consciousness was pulled into a tunnel that led her toward a brilliant light. She could hear her dead grandmother calling her. Once she reached the light, she found other deceased friends and relatives waiting for her there. They refused to let her travel further, even though she wanted to continue into the light. After a joyful reunion, her deceased uncle Gene guided her back to her body. She didn't want to reenter it, but her uncle pushed her back in.

Afterwards, Pam was able to tell the nurses the conversation she had heard, and could describe the surgical saw and other tools that had been used during her operation.

The entire operation was conducted while Pam was officially dead. It is generally assumed that the mind is a function of the brain. Yet even though all three medical tests showed that Pam's brain was dead, something remained alive to observe and remember every detail of what occurred. Could this have been her soul?[5]

Throughout history, some people have had the ability to receive messages from people who have died. Mediums and channelers are the best-known examples of people who communicate with "the other side." The messages these people receive provide comfort to the bereaved relatives who are suffering from their loss. Unfortunately, though, most of the information that comes across does not contain enough factual information to prove that it came from someone who is dead.

However, there are exceptions. One of the most famous examples of this is the remarkable story of James L. Chaffin. Mr. Chaffin was a North Carolina farmer who died in 1921. In his will, dating from 1905, he left his farm and everything he owned to his third son, Marshall. His widow and three other sons received nothing. The family was not surprised, as Marshall had always been his father's favorite, and they all already knew the contents of the will. Consequently, Marshall took over the farm.

Almost four years later, in June 1925, James, the second son, woke up in the middle of the night with a vivid memory of a dream. In his dream, his father had appeared wearing the long black overcoat that he frequently wore. His father said nothing, but continually pointed to the inside pocket of the overcoat. The apparition appeared in another dream, and this time James's father spoke: "You will find my will in my overcoat pocket."

The next morning, James's mother told him that she'd given the coat to his older brother, John. James immediately went to John's house, some twenty miles away. John was not in, but his wife found the coat, which was too big for John to wear. They examined the coat and found that the inside pocket had been sewn up. They cut it open and found a roll of paper tied up with string. James recognized his father's handwriting. He had written: "Read the 27th chapter of Genesis in my daddie's old Bible." James and his sister-in-law looked up the passage in her bible. The 27th chapter of Genesis told how Jacob received his father's blessing and his brother Esau's birthright.

The bible was a family heirloom and was kept at the old Chaffin farmhouse. James took his daughter and two other witnesses with him to examine the bible. At the 27th chapter, they found a sheet of paper with a message written in James's father's handwriting. It read:

After reading the 27th chapter of Genesis, I, James L. Chaffin, do make my last will and testament, and here it is. I want, after giving my body a decent burial, my little property to be equally divided among my four children, if they are living at my death, both personal and real estate divided equal, if not living with share going to their children. And if she is living, you all must take care of your mammy. Now this is my last will and testament. Witness my hand and seal.

James L. Chaffin

This January 16, 1919

Marshall, who had been the sole beneficiary of the 1905 will, was dead by the time the second will was found. His widow recognized her father-in-law's handwriting and agreed that the second will was valid. However, she and her son contested the will in court. Fortunately for the family, an unwitnessed will was considered valid in North Carolina at that time. One week before the court hearing, James saw his father again in a dream. This time his father asked, "Where is my old will?" James took this as a sign that they'd win the case.

The second will was presented in court, and ten witnesses declared that the handwriting was genuine. The court ordered the first will to be canceled, and the second will was duly probated.[6]

This is a remarkable story. Where did the information that came to James Chaffin in his dreams come from, if not from the soul of his father? It's interesting that the son was directed to the overcoat rather than the will. The apparition in the dream told James that the will was in the overcoat. Obviously, the father's memory was faulty. If anything, this adds credibility to the account. The fact that the father returned one week before the trial shows that he was still concerned about the injustice he had unintentionally caused his family. This must be one of the few occasions in which an apparition caused a court to reverse a previous decision.

The evidence of so many near-death experiences from all around the world strongly indicates that we do not die, but transition to an afterlife. As our physical bodies are discarded and remain, it's our souls that move on and return temporarily to the realm of spirit before coming back to give birth to our new incarnations. I find this an incredibly exciting thought. If everyone accepted this, no one would fear death, as they'd know that the end of this lifetime is merely a transition into a whole new stage of life.

I hope this book has given you insights into your soul and enabled you to utilize it to enhance every aspect of your life. Learning your soul's purpose will help you gain a greater appreciation of your particular skills and talents. You'll be more tolerant of people who are traveling on rays that are different from yours, as you'll be able to recognize the specific ray qualities they have brought into this incarnation. You'll also realize that you are a divine being.

What you learn about your past lifetimes will help you understand why you are the specific person you are today. It may reveal and clarify areas of difficulty you have had. Once you understand them, the problems are much easier to deal with, and frequently resolve themselves.

Most importantly, this book will help you to value, appreciate, and nurture your immortal soul. When you do this, you'll become more accepting and loving, your happiness and self-esteem will grow, and you'll gain insights into how you may progress further in this incarnation. You'll also lose all fear of death, as you'll have complete faith in the process of life.

I wish you all the best as you gain a closer connection with the Divine by exploring the miracle of your eternal soul.

SUGGESTED READING

Aristotle. *De Anima (On the Soul)*. Written 350 BCE. Many versions available. Can be found on the Internet at http://classics.mit.edu/Aristotle/soul.html.

Atwater, P. M. H. *Beyond the Light: The Mysteries and Revelations of Near-Death Experiences*. New York: Avon Books, 1994.

———. *We Live Forever: The Real Truth about Death*. Virginia Beach: A.R.E. Press, 2004.

Auerbach, Loyd. *Reincarnation, Channeling and Possession: A Parapsychologist's Handbook*. New York: Warner Books, 1993.

Aurobindo, Sri. *The Problem of Rebirth*. Pondicherry, India: Sri Aurobindo Ashram, 1972.

Bacci, Ingrid, PhD. *The Art of Effortless Living*. London: Bantam Books, 2002.

Baggini, Julian, and Jeremy Stangroom. *Great Thinkers A–Z*. London: Continuum, 2004.

Bailey, Alice A. *A Treatise on the Seven Rays*. New York: Lucis Publishing Company, 1936.

Bertholet, Alfred. *Transmigration of Souls*. London: Harper and Brothers, 1909.

Casey, John. *After Lives: A Guide to Heaven, Hell & Purgatory*. New York: Oxford University Press, 2009.

Cayce, Edgar. *Edgar Cayce on Atlantis*. New York: Paperback Library, 1968.

Cerminara, Gina. *Many Mansions*. New York: William Sloane Associates, 1950.

———. *The World Within*. New York: William Sloane Associates, 1957.

Challoner, H. K. *The Wheel of Rebirth*. Wheaton, IL: Theosophical Publishing House, 1969.

Cornillier, Pierre-Emile. *The Survival of the Soul and Its Evolution after Death*. London: Kegan Paul, Trench, Trubner & Co., 1921.

Crawley, A. E. *The Idea of the Soul*. London: Adam & Charles Black, 1909.

Cullmann, Oscar. *Immortality of the Soul or Resurrection of the Dead?* London: Epworth Press, 1958.

Currie, Ian. *You Cannot Die: The Incredible Findings of a Century of Research on Death*. Toronto: Somerville House

Publishing, 1978. Reprint, Rockport, MA: Element, 1995.

Dale, Cyndi. *The Complete Book of Chakra Healing: Activate the Transformative Power of Your Energy Centers*. Rev. ed. Woodbury, MN: Llewellyn Publications, 2009.

Danelek, J. Allan. *The Mystery of Reincarnation*. Saint Paul, MN: Llewellyn Publications, 2005.

Dennett, Daniel C. *Breaking the Spell: Religion as a Natural Phenomenon*. New York: Viking Penguin, 2006.

Favero, Kevin T. *The Science of the Soul: Scientific Evidence of Human Souls*. Edina, MN: Beaver's Pond Press, 2004.

Fiore, Edith. *You Have Been Here Before*. London: Sphere Books, 1980.

Fisher, Joe. *The Case for Reincarnation*. Toronto: Somerville House Publishing, 1998.

Fodor, Nandor. *Between Two Worlds*. West Nyack, NY: Parker Publishing Co., 1964.

Frazer, J. G. *The Belief in Immortality and the Worship of the Dead*. London: Macmillan and Company, 1929. Reprint, New York: Barnes & Noble, 1969.

Gallup, George, with William Proctor. *Adventures in Immortality*. New York: McGraw-Hill, 1982.

González-Wippler, Migene. *What Happens After Death: Scientific & Personal Evidence for Survival*. Saint Paul, MN: Llewellyn Publications, 1997.

Harpur, Patrick. *A Complete Guide to the Soul*. London: Rider Books, 2010.

Hastings, Adrian, Alistair Mason, and Hugh Pyper, eds. *The Oxford Companion to Christian Thought*. Oxford: Oxford University Press, 2000.

Head, Joseph, and S. L. Cranston, eds. *Reincarnation: An East-West Anthology*. New York: Julian Press, 1961.

Heath, Pamela Rae, and Jon Klimo. *Handbook to the Afterlife*. Berkeley, CA: North Atlantic Books, 2010.

Hodson, Geoffrey. *Reincarnation: Fact or Fallacy?* Wheaton, IL: Theosophical Publishing House, 1967.

Holland, John. *Power of the Soul: Inside Wisdom for an Outside World*. Carlsbad, CA: Hay House, 2007.

Johnson, Raynor. *The Imprisoned Splendour*. London: Hodder & Stoughton, 1953.

Johnson, W. J. *Oxford Dictionary of Hinduism*. Oxford: Oxford University Press, 2009.

Kenny, Dennis. *Promise of the Soul*. New York: John Wiley & Sons, 2002.

Langley, Noel. *Edgar Cayce on Reincarnation*. New York: Paperback Library, 1967.

Long, Jeffrey, MD, with Paul Perry. *Evidence of the Afterlife*. New York: HarperCollins, 2010.

MacGregor, Geddes. *Reincarnation in Christianity*. Wheaton, IL: Quest Books, 1978.

McColman, Carl. *Spirituality: Where Body and Soul Encounter the Sacred*. Georgetown, MA: North Star Publications, 1997.

Merton, Thomas. *Contemplative Prayer*. New York: Doubleday & Company, 1989.

Moody, Raymond. *Life After Life*. Atlanta, GA: Mockingbird Books, 1975.

Moore, Thomas. *Care of the Soul: A Guide for Cultivating Depth and Sacredness in Everyday Life*. New York: HarperCollins, 1992.

———. *The Soul's Religion*. New York: HarperCollins, 2002.

Mumford, Dr. Jonn. *Death: Beginning or End?* Saint Paul, MN: Llewellyn Publications, 1999.

Myss, Caroline. *Anatomy of the Spirit: The Seven Stages of Power and Healing*. New York: Harmony Books, 1996.

Newton, Michael, PhD. *Destiny of Souls: New Case Studies of Life Between Lives*. Saint Paul, MN: Llewellyn Publications, 2000.

———. *Journey of Souls: Case Studies of Life Between Lives*. Saint Paul, MN: Llewellyn Publications, 1994.

———. *Life Between Lives: Hypnotherapy for Spiritual Regression*. Saint Paul, MN: Llewellyn Publications, 2004.

Pond, David. *Western Seeker, Eastern Paths: Exploring Buddhism, Hinduism, Taoism & Tantra*. Saint Paul, MN: Llewellyn Publications, 2003.

Potter, Richard N. *Authentic Spirituality: The Direct Path to Consciousness*. Saint Paul, MN: Llewellyn Publications, 2004.

Rogo, D. Scott. *Life After Death: The Case for Survival of Bodily Death*. Wellingborough: Aquarian Press, 1986.

Russell, Bertrand. *A History of Western Philosophy*. London: George Allen & Unwin, 1946. Revised edition 1961.

Sheed, F. J. *Theology for Beginners*. London: Sheed and Ward, 1958.

Singer, June. *Boundaries of the Soul*. London: Victor Gollancz Limited, 1973.

Steiner, Rudolf. *Life Between Death and Rebirth*. New York: Anthroposophic Press, 1968.

Stevenson, Ian. *Twenty Cases Suggestive of Reincarnation*. Second edition. Charlottesville, VA: University of Virginia Press, 1974.

Thaler, Linda Kaplan, and Robin Koval. *The Power of Nice: How to Conquer the Business World with Kindness*. New York: Doubleday, 2006.

Trainor, Kevin, ed. *Buddhism: The Illustrated Guide*. London: Duncan Baird Publishers, 2001. Revised edition 2004.

Varghese, Roy Abraham, ed. *Great Thinkers on Great Questions*. Oxford: Oneworld Publications, 1998.

Walker, Benjamin. *Encyclopedia of Esoteric Man*. London: Routledge & Kegan Paul, 1977.

Weatherhead, Leslie D. *Psychology in Service of the Soul*. London: Epworth Press, 1929.

Webster, Richard. *The Complete Book of Auras*. Woodbury, MN: Llewellyn Publications, 2010.

———. *Practical Guide to Past-Life Memories: Twelve Proven Methods.* Saint Paul, MN: Llewellyn Publications, 2001.

———. *Soul Mates: Understanding Relationships Across Time.* Saint Paul, MN: Llewellyn Publications, 2001.

Wilson, Colin. *After Life: Survival of the Soul.* Saint Paul, MN: Llewellyn Publications, 2000.

Zukav, Gary. *The Seat of the Soul.* New York: Free Press, 1989.

———. *Soul to Soul: Communications from the Heart.* New York: Free Press, 2007.

NOTES

Introduction

1. Pamela Rae Heath and Jon Klimo, *Handbook to the Afterlife* (Berkeley, CA: North Atlantic Books, 2010), 47.

2. W. Stainton Moses, *Spirit Teachings* (London: Spiritualist Alliance, 1883). *Spirit Teachings* is also available at www .meilach.com/spiritual/books/st/spteach.htm.

3. J. F. Crehan, "Immortality," *Man, Myth & Magic* (London: Marshall Cavendish Corporation, 1970), 4:1413.

4. Bertrand Russell, *A History of Western Philosophy*, rev. ed. (London: George Allen & Unwin, 1961), 249.

5. St. Thomas Aquinas, *Summa Theologica* (*Summary of Theology*)(1264–1274). Many translations are available on the Internet, including www.op.org/summa. Question 75 relates purely to the soul.

6. Edward B. Tylor, *Primitive Culture, Volume 1* (London: John Murray, 1871), 429.

7. Carl Jung quoted in Erwin Schrödinger's *What Is Life? With Mind and Matter and Autobiographical Sketches* (Cambridge: Cambridge University Press, 2006), 119. *What Is Life?* was originally published in 1944.

Chapter One

1. There are many books that recount instances of people remembering their previous incarnations. These include *Reincarnation: Amazing True Cases from Around the World* by Roy Sternman (London: Piatkus Books, 1997) and *Twenty Cases Suggestive of Reincarnation* by Dr. Ian Stevenson, 2nd ed. (Charlottesville, VA: University of Virginia Press, 1974).

2. Stevenson, *Twenty Cases Suggestive of Reincarnation*, 101.

3. Ibid., 91–105.

4. Fred Ayer, Jr., *Before the Colors Fade: Portrait of a Soldier, George S. Patton* (New York: Houghton Mifflin, 1964).

5. This poem can be found in many place on the Internet, including www.mylot.com/w/discussions/1163967.aspx.

6. Stevenson, *Twenty Cases Suggestive of Reincarnation*, 259–69.

7. Edgar Cayce quoted in Benjamin Walker's *Masks of the Soul* (Wellingborough: Aquarian Press, 1981), 50–51.

8. Edgar Cayce, *Edgar Cayce on Atlantis* (New York: Paperback Library, 1968), 150.

9. Charles C. Emerson, "Notes from the Journal of a Scholar," *The Dial*, July 1840. Reprinted in *The Dial: A Magazine for Literature, Philosophy, and Religion*, vol. 1 (Boston, MA: James Munroe and Company, 1841), 14.

10. Richard Webster, *Practical Guide to Past-Life Memories: Twelve Proven Methods* (Saint Paul, MN: Llewellyn Publications, 2001). This book contains a number of different methods to retrieve past-life memories.

11. Noel Langley, *Edgar Cayce on Reincarnation* (New York: Castle Books, 1967), 75.

Chapter Two

1. William Faulkner, speech in *Les Prix Nobel en 1950* (Stockholm, Sweden: P. A. Norstedt & Söner, 1951), 71.

2. Wayne W. Dyer, *Wisdom of the Ages: 60 Days to Enlightenment* (New York: HarperCollins, 1998), 146.

3. Maurice B. Forman, ed., *The Letters of John Keats* (London: Oxford University Press, 1931), 335–36.

4. Ralph Waldo Emerson quoted in *Reincarnation: An East-West Anthology*, compiled and edited by Joseph Head and S. L. Cranston (New York: Julian Press, 1961), 237–38.

5. Jeffrey Burton Russell, *A History of Heaven* (Princeton, NJ: Princeton University Press, 1997), 15.

6. St. Teresa of Ávila quoted in *Interior Castle,* translated from Spanish and edited by E. Allison Peers (London: Sheed & Ward, 1974), I,i,4.

7. Ralph McInerny, "The Existence of the Soul," *Great Thinkers on Great Questions*, edited by Roy Abraham Varghese (Oxford, UK: Oneworld Publications, 1998), 51–52.

8. Joseph Head and S. L. Cranston, eds., *Reincarnation in World Thought* (New York: Julian Press, 1967), 92.

9. Kevin Trainor, ed., *Buddhism: The Illustrated Guide*, rev. ed. (London: Duncan Baird Publishers, 2004), 70.

10. Homer Smith, *Man and His Gods* (Boston, MA: Little, Brown and Company, 1952), 24.

11. Gerald Massey, *The Seven Souls of Man and Their Culmination in Christ* (privately printed, 1900). Available at http://www.africawithin.com/massey/gml1_seven.htm. Also in H. P. Blavatsky, *The Secret Doctrine*, vol. 2 (1888), 632.

12. Daniel C. Dennett, *Breaking the Spell: Religion as a Natural Phenomenon* (New York: Viking Penguin, 2006), 97–98.

13. Alvin Plantinga, "The Existence of the Soul," *Great Thinkers on Great Questions*, edited by Roy Abraham Varghese (Oxford, UK: Oneworld Publications, 1998), 45–46.

Chapter Three

1. Ursula Roberts, *The Mystery of the Human Aura* (London: The Spiritualist Association of Great Britain, 1950), 1.

2. Cassandra Eason, *Encyclopedia of Magic & Ancient Wisdom* (London: Judy Piatkus Ltd., 2000), 11.

3. These three Bible passages appear to relate to auras:

   "And when Aaron and all the children of Israel saw Moses, behold, the skin of his face shone; and they were afraid to come nigh him" (Exodus 34:30).

   At the Transfiguration of Christ, Matthew wrote that Jesus's "face did shine as the sun, and his raiment was white as the light" (Matthew 17:2).

   When Saul was traveling on the road to Damascus "suddenly there shined round about him a light from heaven" (Acts 9:3).

4. Barbara G. Walker, *The Woman's Encyclopedia of Myths and Secrets* (San Francisco, CA: Harper & Row, 1983), 253.

5. Alice A. Bailey, *A Treatise on the Seven Rays* (New York: Lucis Publishing Company, 1936), 42.

Chapter Five

1. Elisabeth Goldsmith, *Ancient Pagan Symbols* (Berwick, ME: Ibis Press, 2003), 206. First published in 1929.

2. W. Wynn Westcott, *Numbers: Their Occult Power and Mystic Virtues* (1890; reprint, London: Theosophical Publishing House, 1974), 73.

3. Rudolph Brasch, *The Supernatural and You!* (Stanmore: Cassell Australia, 1976), 53.

4. Adrian Room, ed., *Brewer's Dictionary of Phrase and Fable* (1870; reprint, London: Cassell & Co, 1999), 1066.

The seven joys of the Virgin Mary are the Annunciation, the Visitation, the Nativity, the Epiphany, the Finding in the Temple, the Resurrection, and the Ascension. The seven sorrows of the Virgin Mary are Simeon's prophecy, the flight into Egypt, the loss of the Holy Child, meeting Jesus Christ on the road to Calvary, the crucifixion, taking Jesus down from the cross, and the entombment. The seven spiritual works of mercy are to tend the sick, feed the hungry, give drink to the thirsty, clothe the naked, befriend the stranger, minister to prisoners, and bury the dead (Matthew 25:35–45). The seven words from the cross are: (1) "Father, forgive them; for they know not what they do" (Luke 23:34); (2) "Today shalt thou be with me in paradise" (Luke 23:43); (3) "Woman, behold thy son! ... Behold thy mother!" (John 19:26–27); (4) "My God, my God, why hast thou forsaken me?" (Matthew 27:46); (5) "I thirst" (John 19:28); (6) "It is finished" (John 19:30); (7) "Father, into thy hands I commend my spirit" (Luke 23:46).

5. *Sepher Yetzirah* quoted in John Michael Greer's *The New Encyclopedia of the Occult* (Saint Paul, MN: Llewellyn Publications, 2003), 431.

6. W. Wynn Westcott, trans., *Sepher Yetzirah* (1887), chapter 4, page 3. Many versions are available. It can also be found at www.sacred-texts.com/jud/yetzirah.htm.

7. Rabbi Geoffrey W. Dennis, *The Encyclopedia of Jewish Myth, Magic and Mysticism* (Woodbury, MN: Llewellyn Publications, 2007), 186.

8. Ute Possekel, *Evidence of Greek Philosophical Concepts in the Writings of Ephrem the Syrian* (Leuven, Belgium: Peeters Publishers, 1999), 191.

9. Adrian Room, ed., *Brewer's Dictionary of Phrase and Fable* (1870; reprint, London: Cassell & Co, 1999), 1068.

10. Ecclesiasticus, also known as The Wisdom of Ben Sira and Sirach, is available in many editions. It can also be found at www.sacred-texts.com/bib/poly/sir.htm.

11. Ernest Busenbark, *Symbols, Sex, and the Stars in Popular Beliefs* (New York: The Truth Seeker Co., 1949), 243.

Chapter Seven

1. Cyndi Dale, *The Complete Book of Chakra Healing: Activate the Transformative Power of Your Energy Centers*, rev. ed. (Woodbury, MN: Llewellyn Publications, 2009), 233.

Chapter Eight

1. St. Thomas Aquinas quoted in James V. Schall's *Roman Catholic Political Philosophy* (Lanham, MD: Lexington Books, 2004), 186.

Chapter Nine

1. Robert Browning quoted in F. E. Halliday's *Robert Browning: His Life and Work* (London: Jupiter Books, 1975), 74.

2. Victor Basch, translated by Catherine Alison Phillips, *Schumann: A Life of Suffering* (New York: Alfred A. Knopf, 1931), 230. This book can be found at http://www.archive.org/stream/schumannalifeofs027254mbp/schumannalifeofs027254mbp_djvu.txt.

Chapter Ten

1. Carl Jung quoted in Erwin Schrödinger's *What Is Life? With Mind and Matter and Autobiographical Sketches* (Cambridge: Cambridge University Press, 2006), 119. *What Is Life?* was originally published in 1944.

2. Will Johnson, *Rumi: Gazing at the Beloved* (Rochester, VT: Inner Traditions, 2003).

3. Dr. Bruce Arroll quoted in Geraldine Johns's "Fighting 'Toxic Uncertainty,'" *New Zealand Listener*, 230, no. 3722 (September 10, 2011): 24–26.

4. Melissa B. Wanzer quoted in "Laughter is the Best Medicine," *ScienceDaily*, January 26, 2008. Also available at www.sciencedaily.com/releases/2008/01/080124200913.htm.

Conclusion

1. Jeffrey Long, MD, with Paul Perry, *Evidence of the Afterlife* (New York: HarperCollins, 2010), 5.

2. Pamela Rae Heath and Jon Klimo, *Handbook to the Afterlife* (Berkeley, CA: North Atlantic Books, 2010), 56.

3. George Gallup, with William Proctor, *Adventures in Immortality* (New York: McGraw-Hill, 1982), 32.

4. Caresse Crosby, *The Passionate Years* (New York: The Dial Press, 1953), 18–19.

5. Michael Sabom, MD, *Light and Death* (Grand Rapids, MI: Zondervan, 1998). See also www.near-death.com /experiences/evidence01.html.

6. *Proceedings of the Society for Psychical Research*, 36, (1927): 517–24. The story of the Chaffin will can be found in many books, including George Nugent Merle Tyrrell's *Science and Psychical Phenomena (Perspectives in Psychical Research)* (Secaucus, NJ: University Books, 1961), 28–30.

INDEX

To Write to the Author

If you wish to contact the author or would like more information about this book, please write to the author in care of Llewellyn Worldwide and we will forward your request. Both the author and the publisher appreciate hearing from you and learning of your enjoyment of this book and how it has helped you. Llewellyn Worldwide cannot guarantee that every letter written to the author can be answered, but all will be forwarded. Please write to:

Richard Webster
% Llewellyn Worldwide
2143 Wooddale Drive, Dept. 978-0-7387-3249-7
Woodbury, MN 55125-2989

Please enclose a self-addressed stamped envelope for reply, or $1.00 to cover costs. If outside the U.S.A., enclose an international postal reply coupon.

GET MORE AT LLEWELLYN.COM

Visit us online to browse hundreds of our books and decks, plus sign up to receive our e-newsletters and exclusive online offers.

- **Free tarot readings • Spell-a-Day • Moon phases**
- **Recipes, spells, and tips • Blogs • Encyclopedia**
- **Author interviews, articles, and upcoming events**

GET SOCIAL WITH LLEWELLYN

Find us on Facebook
www.Facebook.com/LlewellynBooks

Follow us on

www.Twitter.com/Llewellynbooks

GET BOOKS AT LLEWELLYN

LLEWELLYN ORDERING INFORMATION

Order online: Visit our website at www.llewellyn.com to select your books and place an order on our secure server.

Order by phone:
- Call toll free within the U.S. at 1-877-NEW-WRLD (1-877-639-9753)
- Call toll free within Canada at 1-866-NEW-WRLD (1-866-639-9753)
- We accept VISA, MasterCard, and American Express

Order by mail:
Send the full price of your order (MN residents add 6.875% sales tax) in U.S. funds, plus postage and handling to: Llewellyn Worldwide, 2143 Wooddale Drive Woodbury, MN 55125-2989

POSTAGE AND HANDLING

STANDARD (U.S. & Canada):
(Please allow 12 business days)
$25.00 and under, add $4.00.
$25.01 and over, FREE SHIPPING.

INTERNATIONAL ORDERS (airmail only):
$16.00 for one book, plus $3.00 for each additional book.

Visit us online for more shipping options.
Prices subject to change.

FREE CATALOG!

To order, call
1-877-
NEW-WRLD
ext. 8236
or visit our
website

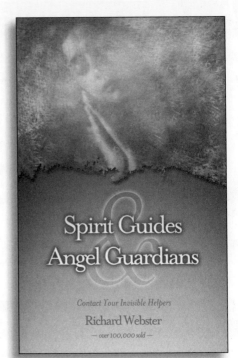

Spirit Guides
&
Angel Guardians

Contact Your Invisible Helpers

Richard Webster

— *over 100,000 sold* —

Spirit Guides & Angel Guardians

Contact Your Invisible Helpers

RICHARD WEBSTER

They come to our aid when we least expect it, and they disappear as soon as their work is done. Invisible helpers are available to all of us; in fact, we all regularly receive messages from our guardian angels and spirit guides but usually fail to recognize them. This book will help you to realize when this occurs. And when you carry out the exercises provided, you will be able to communicate freely with both your guardian angels and spirit guides.

You will see your spiritual and personal growth take a huge leap forward as soon as you welcome your angels and guides into your life. This book contains numerous case studies that show how angels have touched the lives of others, just like yourself. Experience more fun, happiness, and fulfillment than ever before. Other people will also notice the difference as you become calmer, more relaxed, and more loving than ever before.

978-1-56718-795-3, 368 pp., $5^3/_{16}$ x 8   **$12.95**

Creative
Visualization

For Beginners

Achieve Your Goals & Make Your Dreams Come True

RICHARD WEBSTER

Creative Visualization for Beginners

Achieve Your Goals & Make Your Dreams Come True

RICHARD WEBSTER

Everyone has the natural ability to visualize success, but ordinary methods used to reach fulfillment can be inefficient and unclear. Creative visualization allows anyone to change the direction of his or her life by mentally picturing and altering images of their goals. In his popular conversational style, bestselling author Richard Webster explains the methodology behind creative visualization, and provides readers with the tools and knowledge necessary to achieve their goals in all areas of life, including business, health, self-improvement, relationships, and nurturing and restoring the soul.

Creative Visualization for Beginners includes simple exercises enhanced by real-life situations from the author's personal experiences with creative visualization, and demonstrates how to react when you encounter difficulties along the way. In addition, he gives advice on what to do if you have no predetermined goals in mind, and how to implement positive results while maintaining your natural balance.

978-0-7387-0807-2, 264 pp., 5³/₁₆ x 8   **$13.95**

Pendulum Magic

For Beginners

Tap Into Your Inner Wisdom

RICHARD WEBSTER

Pendulum Magic for Beginners

Tap Into Your Inner Wisdom

RICHARD WEBSTER

The pendulum is a simple, accurate, and versatile device consisting of a weight attached to a chain or thread. Arguably the most underrated item in the magician's arsenal, the pendulum can reveal information not found any other way. It can read energy patterns, extracting information from deep inside our subconscious.

This book will teach you how to perform apparent miracles such as finding lost objects, helping your potted plants grow better, protecting yourself from harmful foods, detecting dishonesty in others, and even choosing the right neighborhood. Explore past lives, recall dreams, release blocks to achieving happiness, and send your wishes out into the universe.

978-0-7387-0192-9, 240 pp., 5³/₁₆ x 8   **$13.95**

RICHARD WEBSTER

THE COMPLETE BOOK OF

AURAS

Learn to See, Read, Strengthen & Heal Auras

The Complete Book of Auras

Learn to See, Read, Strengthen & Heal Auras

RICHARD WEBSTER

Everything you ever wanted to know about the aura is now in one easy-to-use guidebook!

Bestselling author Richard Webster shares simple, step-by-step techniques for seeing, feeling, strengthening, and cleansing the aura—your personal energetic signature—for better health, psychic protection, and achieving your highest goals. Learn to balance and clear the seven chakras using pendulums and crystals. Practice enjoyable meditations, visualizations, and other practical aura-based methods. Learn to recognize signs of illness, release emotional blockages, and determine anyone's mood, personality, and true nature just by their aura's appearance.

This book also offers expert instruction on giving insightful aura readings—and even how to read the auras of pets.

978-0-7387-2180-4, 216 pp., 6 x 9   **$16.95**

To order, call 1-877-NEW-WRLD
Prices subject to change without notice
Order at Llewellyn.com 24 hours a day, 7 days a week!